HIDDEN
LONDON

Discover Over 100 of the City's Hidden Attractions

David Hampshire

London Borough of Southwa...

Isambard Kingdom
Brunel
1806-1859

Great Victorian Engine...

His first project was the Than...
Tunnel, the world's first
underwater tunnel

Voted by the People

T0163121

City Books • Bath • England

First published 2012 as London's Hidden Secrets Volume 2
Second Edition 2020

Copyright © Survival Books 2020
Cover design: Herring Bone Design
Cover photo: London from the Shard © fuseboy (Adobe Stock)
Maps © Jim Watson

City Books, c/o Survival Books Limited
Office 169, 3 Edgar Buildings
George Street, Bath BA1 2FJ, United Kingdom
+44 (0)1305-266918
info@survivalbooks.net
citybooks.co, survivalbooks.net and londons-secrets.com

British Library Cataloguing in Publication Data
A CIP record for this book is available
from the British Library

ISBN: 978-1-913171-20-9

Printed in China

Acknowledgements

We've been the fortunate recipients of much help, support and enthusiasm in researching and writing this book. In addition to the many photographers – whose beautiful images bring London to life – we would like to heartily thank the following, in no particular order: Lisa Miller (RGS), Robert Waite (Bruce Castle), Helen Walker (Pitzhanger Manor), Karen Johnson (English Heritage), Vanda Foster (Gunnersbury Park Museum), Mark de Novellis (Orleans House Gallery), Vicky Carroll (William Morris Gallery), Julia Walton (Harrow School), Maurice Bitton (Bevis Marks), Martin Sach (Canal Museum), Kevin Brown (Alexander Fleming Museum), Anita O'Brien (Cartoon Museum), Diane Clements (Museum of Freemasonry), Darren T (Magic Circle), Jesse Bela Sullivan (Marx Memorial Library), Nicola Kalimeris (Museum of London), Elizabeth Armati (Mansion House), Francesca Brooks (Saatchi Gallery), Victoria Sanderson (Forty Hall), Robert Hulse (Brunel Museum), Dudley Smith (Wimbledon Windmill & Museum), Richard Meunier (Royal London Hospital Museum), Verya Daleri (York House Gardens), Glyn Williams (St Augustine Church), David Hamilton Peters (St James's Church), Fiona (St Mary's Church), Bruna (St Peter's Italian Church), Mary O'Neill (St George the Martyr), Amanda Siravo (Brompton Oratory), Ian Henghes (Waterlow Park), Stephen Evans (St Marylebone Church) and David Bentley (Golders Hill Park Zoo).

Last but not least, special thanks are due to Robbi Atilgan for editing, Susan Griffith for final proof checking, John Marshall for desktop publishing and photo selection; David Gillingwater for the cover design, Jim Watson for the superb maps, and the author's partner (Alexandra) for the constant supply of tea and coffee.

NOTE

Before visiting anywhere featured in this book it's advisable to check the opening times, which are liable to change without notice.

Contents

Introduction

L ondon has a fascinating and turbulent 2,000-year history, during which it has been burnt down several times, rebuilt, bombed in two world wars and rebuilt again. Despite, the ravages of time and conflicts (and developers!), the city has enough world-famous attractions to keep the average visitor or resident occupied for a month of Sundays, which are more than adequately covered in a wealth of guidebooks. What *Hidden London* does is take you off the beaten path – side-stepping the city's tourist-clogged major sights – to seek out its more unusual charms and esoteric, mysterious side.

Like our sister publications, *London's Hidden Secrets* and *London's Secret Places*, *Hidden London* contains a wealth of unusual, hidden and little-known attractions. Among the over 100 places featured are an abundance of historic churches and other ancient buildings; secret gardens and magnificent Victorian cemeteries; fascinating small museums and galleries; characterful pubs and stunning hotels; cutting-edge art and design, and much more.

Inside you'll discover a lovely church in the shadow of Westminster Abbey where William Caxton and Sir Walter Raleigh are buried, and Sir Winston Churchill was married; an atmospheric 17th-century public house where Mark Twain, Sir Arthur Conan Doyle, Dr Samuel Johnson and Charles Dickens (among others) were frequent visitors; a splendid 16th-century hall where Shakespeare's *Twelfth Night* was first performed; an absorbing museum dedicated to a 'secret' society that numbered Edward VII and Sir Winston Churchill among its members; and a majestic Victorian cemetery where Sir Henry Doulton, Baron Julius de Reuter and Sir Henry Tate are buried.

Hidden London isn't intended as a walking guide, although many of the places covered are close to one another in central London – notably in the hubs of Westminster and the City – where you can easily stroll between them, while some are out in the suburbs. However, most are close to public transport links and relatively easy to get to. What's more the vast majority are free, so there's no excuse for not getting out there and exploring.

With a copy of *Hidden London* to hand to inspire you, you need never be bored of London (or life). We hope you enjoy discovering the city's 'secrets' as much as we did.

David Hampshire
December 2019

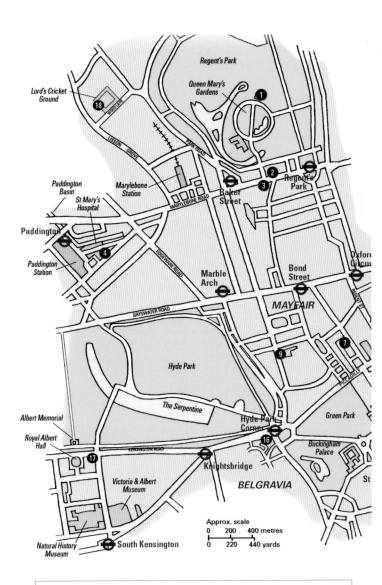

1. St John's Lodge Garden
2. Royal Academy of Music Museum
3. St Marylebone
4. Alexander Fleming Museum
5. Soho Square Garden
6. London Transport Museum
7. Faraday Museum at the Royal Institution
8. St Clement Danes
9. Mount Street Gardens
10. St James's, Piccadilly
11. Marlborough House
12. Institute of Contemporary Arts
13. Household Cavalry Museum
14. St Margaret's Church
15. Jewel Tower
16. The Grenadier
17. Royal Geographical Society
18. MCC Museum & Tours
19. Cartoon Museum

CHAPTER 1

CITY OF WESTMINSTER

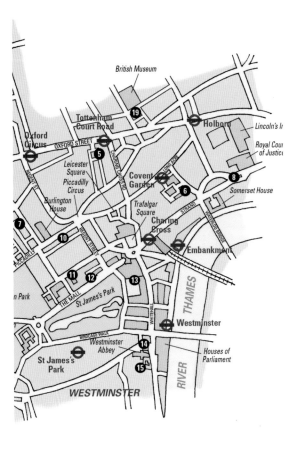

Address: Inner Circle, Regent's Park, NW1 4NX (royalparks.org.uk/parks/ the-regents-park/things-to-see-and-do/gardens-and-landscapes/st.-johns- lodge-gardens)

Opening hours: 7am-dusk

Cost: free

Transport: Baker Street or Regent's Park tube

ST JOHN'S LODGE GARDEN

The garden of St John's Lodge – built in 1817-19 by architect John Raffield for Charles Augustus Tulk, MP – is exquisite; it's the quintessential English garden offering great views of the imposing lodge, which was the first house built in Regent's Park. In 1892, a new garden 'fit for meditation' was designed (for the third Marquess of Bute) with formal areas, a fountain pond, Doric temple, stone portico and partly sunken chapel, which reflected Arts and Crafts ideas and the revival of interest in the classical.

The garden has been open to the public since 1928 and is completely separate from the Lodge and maintained by the Royal Parks. It was renovated and redesigned in 1994 by Landscape Architects Colvin & Moggridge to reflect the original plan and honour the 3rd Marquess of Bute. A new entrance walk was created to the east of the gatehouse and bungalow, with double gates to provide privacy for the house. The east-west scalloped hedge was replanted in yew, but the 1920s flower beds were renewed after public consultation, a variation from the original plan designed by architect, Robert Weir Schultz (1860-1951). New high-backed wooden benches were also commissioned. The new planting established quickly and today the gardens form a luxuriant oasis in the heart of the city.

A metal arbour, reflecting the original stone portico, and a wooden covered seat were created, along with the installation of a number of new statues and urns. Among the fine statues are *Hylas and the Nymph* by Henry Pegram (central in a small pond) – a bronze of a

> The Lodge remained in private hands until 1916 – past owners included Lord Wellesley (1st Duke of Wellington), Sir Isaac Goldsmid and the Marquesses of Bute. Today it's one of only two villas that remain within Regent's Park from John Nash's original conception, and is now leased by Prince Jefri Bolkiah of Brunei.

naked man with a sensual nymph seizing his legs to pull him to his doom – and *The Goatherd's Daughter*, a bronze by Charles L. Hartwell of a semi-draped shepherdess holding a kid-goat with the inscription 'To all protectors of the defenceless.'

In order to enjoy this haven of calm and beauty, you first have to find it! From the Inner Circle, proceed anti-clockwise past Chester Road on your right, and some 200yds further on you'll find the entrance to St John's Lodge Garden on the right via a paved arbour pathway.

Address: Marylebone Road, NW1 5HT (020-7873 7373, ram.ac.uk/museum)

Opening hours: Mon-Fri 11.30am-5.30pm, Sat noon to 4pm, closed Sun

Cost: free

Transport: Baker Street or Regent's Park tube

ROYAL ACADEMY OF MUSIC MUSEUM

The Royal Academy of Music was founded in 1822 by Lord Burghersh (1784-1859) and was granted its Royal Charter in 1830 by George IV. It moved to its current, custom-built premises in Marylebone Road in 1911. The museum is situated in the York Gate building, linked to the Academy's building via a basement, designed in 1822 by John Nash (1752-1835) as part of the main entrance to Regent's Park.

The Academy (as it's usually called) is Britain's oldest degree-granting music school and has been a college of the University of London since 1999. It's the country's foremost specialist higher education institution and also number one for music, in addition to being Britain's leading conservatoire. Throughout its almost 200-year history it has trained thousands of accomplished musicians and has a student body of almost 700 (drawn from over 50 countries) in over 20 musical disciplines.

Many famous musicians – singers, players, conductors and composers – have studied at the Academy, some of whom returned as teachers to stimulate new generations of musicians, while many became leaders in their chosen musical fields

> If you wish to experience the special atmosphere of the Academy, you can drop in for a concert, master class or any public event, most of which are free.

and professions. Among the Academy's most distinguished living alumni are Sir Elton John, Annie Lennox, Michael Nyman, Sir Simon Rattle, while those from previous generations include Sir John Barbirolli, Sir John Tavener, Sir John Dankworth, Sir Arthur Sullivan and Sir Henry Wood (of Proms fame), to name just a few.

The museum displays material from the Academy's world-renowned collection of instruments, manuscripts, paintings, busts, drawings, teaching aids and artefacts, batons, furnishings, memorabilia and other objects. Highlights of the collections include Cremonese stringed instruments from 1650 to 1740, a collection of English pianos from 1790 to 1850 from the famous Mobbs Collection, and original manuscripts by Purcell, Mendelssohn, Liszt, Brahms, Sullivan and Vaughan Williams. An integral part of Academy life, the museum regularly hosts exhibitions and events, including daily piano demonstrations.

Since its foundation the Academy has acquired important musical collections, including many named after individuals such as composer Sir Arthur Sullivan, conductor Sir Henry Wood and the Foyle (Yehudi) Menuhin Archive. The Academy also has a shop, restaurant and a bar open in the evening for drinks and snacks.

AT A GLANCE

Address: 17 Marylebone Road, NW1 5LT (020-7935 7315, stmarylebone. org)

Opening hours: **Mon to Fri 9am-5pm, Sat-Sun 8am-4pm. See website for service times.**

Cost: **free**

Transport: **Baker Street or Regent's Park tube**

ST MARYLEBONE

The present Marylebone church (Church of England) is the fourth to serve the parish, designed by Thomas Hardwicke and consecrated in 1817. It was built over a large vaulted crypt, which served as the parish burial ground until 1853, when the entrance was bricked up and its use discontinued (but later re-opened – see below).

In 1885, major alterations were made including the removal of the end wall, the creation of a chancel for a robed choir and a sanctuary within the new apse. The upper galleries on the sides of the church were removed, revealing the full length of the windows and allowing in more light. New, beautifully-carved mahogany choir stalls with angel ends were installed, the floor was covered with marble mosaic, a fine marble pulpit and two balustrades were constructed, and a gilded cross set into the ceiling above the site of the original altar. The new decorations were in the neo-classical style, combined with the Pre-Raphaelite love of detail, resulting in the magnificent church you see today (although bombing in World War Two blew out the windows).

The church (and previous churches on the site) has many historical links, including the baptism of Lord Byron and

> The church's tranquil churchyard is a haven from the bustle of Marylebone Road and stages the delightfully named 'Cabbages and Frocks' market on Saturdays.

Nelson's daughter, Horatia; the marriage of Sheridan to Miss Linley; and the graves of Charles and Samuel Wesley. Charles Dickens (1812-1870) and his family lived nearby in Devonshire Terrace and his son was baptised here (many characters in David Copperfield were based on people living in Marylebone). The poet Robert Browning and Elizabeth Barrett were secretly married here in 1846 after exchanging 574 love letters, which is commemorated by the Browning Chapel (1949).

The lovely crystal chandeliers were donated in 1968 by the Marylebone Council Chamber after it merged with the City of Westminster. The organ – by the celebrated Austrian firm of Rieger – is one of the finest in the country and is played regularly by Royal Academy of Music students. St Marylebone has long had a reputation for the excellence of its music; there's a professional choir on Sundays and a wealth of concerts and recitals are held throughout the year.

Today the crypt, which was refurbished and opened in 1987 by HRH The Prince of Wales, is surprisingly an NHS (Marylebone) Health Centre, and a centre for physical and spiritual healing. It also contains a chapel and café and stages art exhibitions.

Address: **St Mary's Hospital, Praed Street, W2 1NY (020-3312 6528, imperial.nhs.uk/about-us/who-we-are/fleming-museum)**

Opening hours: **Mon-Thu 10am-1pm (other times by appointment)**

Cost: **adults £4, children, students, senior citizens and the unemployed £2**

Transport: **Paddington tube/rail**

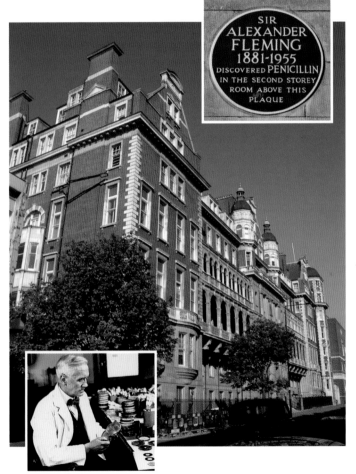

Alexander Fleming

ALEXANDER FLEMING MUSEUM

A museum dedicated to the founder of penicillin might not immediately set the pulse racing, but it tells an engaging story. Alexander Fleming (1881-1955) discovered the antibiotic in 1928 – a breakthrough that revolutionised medicine and earned him a Nobel Prize – in a basic and under-funded laboratory at St Mary's Hospital (founded in 1845). The breakthrough was actually made as a result of an accident when an experiment was mistakenly contaminated, resulting in the discovery of the antibacterial powers of penicillin. "When I awoke just after dawn on September 28, 1928, I certainly didn't plan to revolutionise medicine by discovering the world's first antibiotic or bacteria killer," Fleming would later say, "But I suppose that was exactly what I did." Today there are few lives that haven't been touched by this phenomenal discovery, before which there were no antibiotics and the slightest infection could result in death.

The museum contains a reconstruction of Fleming's restored laboratory, while displays and a video uncover the remarkable story of how a chance discovery became a lifesaving drug destined to revolutionise medicine. There are also exhibits about Fleming himself and his commitment to the further development of his discoveries.

Fleming was born on 6th August 1881 at Lochfield in Ayrshire, Scotland. After attending Kilmarnock Academy he moved to London, where he attended the Regent Street Polytechnic and, after working in a shipping office for four years, was persuaded by his elder brother, Tom (an ophthalmic surgeon), to study medicine. In 1903, he enrolled at St Mary's Hospital Medical School in Paddington and after qualifying joined the research department, where

> Fleming was awarded the Nobel Prize in Physiology or Medicine in 1945, along with Howard Florey and Ernst Boris Chain (who did further research and mass-produced penicillin). He died in London in 1955 and was interred in St Paul's Cathedral.

he became assistant bacteriologist to Sir Almroth Wright (1861-1947), a pioneer in vaccine therapy and immunology.

Fleming served in World War One as a captain in the Royal Army Medical Corps and worked in battlefield hospitals in France, where he discovered that antiseptics were killing more soldiers than infection itself. In 1918 he returned to St Mary's, where he discovered penicillin in 1928. His research was later taken up by Howard Florey and others, enabling the mass-production of penicillin during World War Two, since when it has saved millions of lives around the world.

SOHO SQUARE GARDEN

L aid out in the late 17th century, Soho Square is a garden square – originally called King's Square, after Charles II – which in its early years was one of the most fashionable places to live in London. It was created by the development of Kemps Field by Richard Firth and one of its early residents was the Duke of Monmouth, who – as legend has it – would shout 'So Ho' as he set off for hunting nearby, thus unwittingly dubbing the Square and the surrounding area.

A statue of Charles II by Danish sculptor Caius Gabriel Cibber (1630-1700) was placed at the centre of the Square in 1681, but was removed in 1875 and only returned in 1938.

The garden was first opened to the public in 1954, when the gardens committee leased it to the City of Westminster, which provided the current railings and gates in 1959. It's one of the busiest gardens in Westminster, being located just south of bustling Oxford Street, and is used extensively from morning to night.

The Soho Square neighbourhood is universally regarded as the most prestigious (and expensive) address of London's film and media organisations, which include the British Board of Film Classification, 20th Century Fox and Paul McCartney's MPL Communications. Two of the original houses, numbers 10 and 15, remain, while at numbers 8-9 is the French Protestant church, built in 1891-3,

> The Square is noted for its two-storey, half-timbered, 'gardener's hut' – part tool-shed, part arbour – which is Grade II listed and has been described as 'an octagonal market cross building in the Tudorbethan style.'

and at 21a is St Patrick's Church, a large Roman Catholic parish church featuring catacombs that extend deep under the Square.

Soho Square contains a bench that commemorates the late singer Kirsty MacColl (1959-2000) – killed by a powerboat while diving in Mexico – who wrote the song 'Soho Square' for her album Titanic Days. After her death in 2000, fans dedicated a bench in her honour, inscribing the lyrics 'One day I'll be Waiting There / No Empty Bench in Soho Square.'

The Square is shielded from the business and noise of Oxford Street by the surrounding buildings and, when not full of people, is quiet and relaxing. During the summer it hosts free, open-air concerts and is a popular lunch and picnic spot.

AT A GLANCE

Address: Covent Garden Piazza, WC2E 7BB (020-7379 6344, ltmuseum. co.uk)

Opening hours: 10am-6pm

Cost: adults £18, concessions £17 (£1.50 discount when booking online), under 17s free; tickets are valid for a year

Transport: Covent Garden tube

LONDON TRANSPORT MUSEUM

The London Transport Museum (or LT Museum) preserves and explains London's rich and fascinating transport heritage, and demonstrates how it was integral to London's growth as the world's most influential and iconic city. The majority of the museum's exhibits originated in the collection of London Transport – which was replaced by Transport for London (TfL) in 2000, since when the museum has expanded to cover all aspects of the city's transportation.

The museum is situated in a Victorian iron and glass building, designed as a flower market by William Rogers in 1871, originally part of Covent Garden market (which moved to Nine Elms in 1971). It has been home to the museum since 1980 and underwent a £22 million refurbishment in 2005-2007 to enable the expansion of the collection to encompass the larger remit of TfL.

The first collection was assembled at the beginning of the 20th century by the London General Omnibus Company (LGOC) when it began to preserve buses being retired from service. The LGOC was taken over by the London Electric Railway (LER) and the collection expanded to include rail vehicles; it continued to grow while responsibility for London's public transport passed through various bodies, until being assumed by Transport for London.

There's also an LT Museum Depot in Acton (2 Museum Way, 118-120 Gunnersbury Lane, W3 9BQ) containing 320,000 objects which, although principally a storage site, has regular visitor days and guided tours throughout the year.

The museum contains many examples of buses, trams, trolleybuses and railway vehicles from the 19th and 20th centuries, as well as artefacts and exhibits related to the operation and marketing of passenger services, and the impact that the developing transport network has had on the city and its population.

The museum's highlights include 'London – The First World City', exploring how transport allowed London to become the world's first truly cosmopolitan city; 'Victorian Transport', which details transport innovations that took place in Victorian London; 'World's First Underground', the history of London's groundbreaking tube network; 'Growth of Suburbia', which recounts the growth of suburban London; and 'London in the 1920s and 1930s', which explores the innovation of bus use across the city. The museum also relates how public transport helped London operate throughout two world wars, as well as detailing how modern transport systems work, particularly the technical sophistication of the city's tube network.

The museum also contains a poster collection, library, café and shop.

Address: **21 Albemarle Street, W1S 4BS (020-7409 2992, rigb.org/visit-us/faraday-museum)**

Opening hours: **Mon-Fri 9am-5pm; café Mon-Fri 9am-3.30pm**

Cost: **free**

Transport: **Gren Park tube**

Michael Faraday

FARADAY MUSEUM AT THE ROYAL INSTITUTION

The Faraday Museum, which commemorates the scientific pioneer, Michael Faraday (1791-1867) and showcases his life's work, occupies two rooms in the basement of the old 18th-century Royal Institution building. Faraday is regarded as the 'father of electricity' and a prolific experimenter, whose greatest discoveries include the principles behind the electric motor, the generator and the transformer.

The Royal Institution of Great Britain (usually referred to as the 'Ri') was founded in 1799 for 'diffusing the knowledge, and facilitating the general introduction, of useful mechanical inventions and improvements; and for teaching, by courses of philosophical lectures and experiments, the application of science to the common purposes of life' (phew!). Today the Ri is an independent charity dedicated to connecting people with the world of science through discovery, innovation, inspiration and imagination.

Faraday joined the Ri as a chemical assistant in 1813 and it was here that he conducted most of his work. The highlight of the exhibition is his laboratory as it was in the 1850s – where he discovered electromagnetism in 1831 – which has been reconstructed using contemporary paintings. It contains some of his original equipment, including his first electric generator, magneto-spark apparatus, a large electromagnet, a vacuum pump and jars of chemicals.

The Ri collections include the original apparatus and papers of many notable scientists who researched, lectured and lived in the building, including Sir Humphry Davy (who discovered sodium and potassium), John Tyndall (successor to Faraday), James Dewar (liquefaction), Sir William Lawrence Bragg (who won the Nobel Prize in Physics in 1915 for his work on X-ray diffraction) and George Porter (Nobel Prize in Chemistry 1967). Other famous scientists to pass through the Ri's ranks include T. H. Huxley and Lord Rutherford. In total, 15 scientists attached to the Royal Institution have won Nobel Prizes.

> The Royal Institution is the oldest independent research body in the world – granted a royal charter by George III in 1800.

Throughout its history, the Institution has supported public engagement with science through a programme of lectures, many of which continue today. The most famous of these are the annual Ri Christmas Lectures, inaugurated by Faraday in 1825. If you're interested in how the world works or how to make it work better through science, the Ri is the place for you. More prosaically, but still noteworthy, it also has a restaurant, café and bar.

AT A GLANCE

Address: **Strand, WC2R 1DH** (020-7242 8282, **raf.mod.uk/our-organisation/ units/st-clement-danes-church**)

Opening hours: **Mon-Fri 9am-4pm, Sat 10am-3pm, Sun 9.30am-3pm. See website for service times.**

Cost: **free**

Transport: **Temple tube**

ST CLEMENT DANES

This beautiful church sits isolated on a traffic island in the middle of the Strand, where a church has stood for over 1,000 years; the original was reputedly built by Danes (named after St Clement, patron saint of mariners) expelled from the City of London by King Alfred in the 9th century. It's mentioned in William the Conqueror's Domesday Book (1086) and for almost 150 years was in the care of the Knights Templar (1170-1312). The church escaped damage in the Great Fire (1666) but was rebuilt in 1680-2 by Sir Christopher Wren; the west tower was added by Joshua Marshall in 1669 and the familiar spire by James Gibbs in 1720.

One of London's most beautiful churches, St Clement Danes is flooded by light from the unusually high windows, with clear reamy (mouth-blown) antique glass. The altar and chancel, with their simplicity and beauty, are the focus of worship. The altar is of oak, while immediately above is a reredos adorned by a painting in gold (by Ruskin Spear) of the Annunciation, behind which is a magnificent stained glass window of Christ in Glory by Carl Edwards, all 20th century.

Numerous gifts and memorials received from individuals, organisations and air forces from around the world create the sense of remembrance that is integral to the ethos of the church, including the splendid crests inlaid in the stone floor, worked in brass, copper, white bronze and marble. Outside the church are statues of Lord Dowding, commander of Fighter Command during the Battle of Britain, and Sir Arthur (Bomber) Harris, Marshall of the RAF.

The bells of St Clement (claimed to be those mentioned in the famous nursery rhyme, Oranges and Lemons, which is played here regularly) include the Sanctus Bell, cast in 1588 (the year of the Spanish Armada) by Robert Mot, founder of the Whitechapel Foundry. The gilded organ (which replaced one by Father Smith, destroyed in 1941) – reputedly one of the best in London – was designed by Ralph Downes and made by Harrison and Harrison of Durham, and was a gift from the United States Air Force.

On 10th May 1941, incendiary bombs gutted the building leaving only the walls and tower standing, so ending another chapter in its rich history. In 1953, the church was given to the Air Council and rebuilt after a worldwide appeal, and re-consecrated in 1958 as the Central Church of the Royal Air Force. Today it's a shrine dedicated to all those of the Allied Air Forces who gave their lives during World War Two.

Address: Mount Street, W1K 2TH (westminster.gov.uk/my-parks/parks/mount-street-gardens)

Opening hours: **8am-dusk**

Cost: **free**

Transport: **Green Park or Bond Street tube**

MOUNT STREET GARDENS

Mount Street Gardens are a hidden oasis in Mayfair and although close to Grosvenor Square (and the former American Embassy) are relatively unknown. They're situated on the site of an important early Georgian cemetery, built as a result of the 1711 'Fifty New Churches Act'. The land was acquired by the newly-formed church of St George's Hanover Square as a burial ground in 1723 (closed in 1854). Like many other urban cemeteries and former burial grounds in London, it was later converted into a public garden.

The gardens were laid out in 1889 with plants, paths and a small fountain, and have changed little since their inception, retaining their late 19th-century gate piers at the South Audley Street entrance. The bronze drinking fountain (restored in 2005), located at the east end of the gardens near the beautiful Farm Street Church, depicts a rearing horse and was designed by Sir Ernest George (1839-1922) and Harold Peto (1854-1933) in 1891 for Henry Lofts (a local estate agent). The church (built 1844-1849) is the scene of many society weddings and has a high altar by Augustus Pugin (who designed the interior of the Palace of Westminster).

Planting in the gardens includes mature London plane trees and a variety of smaller trees, shrubs and ornamental flower beds. A microclimate (due to the protection afforded by the buildings which enclose much of the gardens) allows an Australian Mimosa, a Canary Islands Date Palm and three Dawn Redwoods to flourish. Around 90 sponsored benches line the paths, many of which were donated by Americans from the nearby

> During the cold war the gardens were a favourite haunt of KGB spies, who left secret notes in the slats of the garden benches.

former US Embassy (now moved to Nine Elms); inscriptions include 'An American who did not find a park like this in New York City.'

The gardens are designated a 'Site of Importance for Nature Conservation' and are home to various bird species (there's also a bird bath), depicted on a bird life interpretation panel. They won the London Gardens Society 'Public Large Squares Award' in 2002 and have been a Green Flag Award winner annually since 2007. The gardens were restored in 2005 through the efforts of local residents.

Mount Street Gardens are a haven of peace and quiet, and a lovely place to take a break, read or just savour the magical atmosphere, cocooned from the noise and bustle of the surrounding streets.

AT A GLANCE

Address: 197 Piccadilly, W1J 9LL (020-7734 4511, sjp.org.uk)

Opening hours: 8.30am-6.30pm. Unless you wish to listen to a lunchtime recital, it's best to avoid 1.10-2pm Mon, Wed and Fri. See website for service times.

Cost: free

Transport: Piccadilly Circus or Green Park tube

ST JAMES'S, PICCADILLY

St James's is a majestic Anglican parish church on Piccadilly, designed by Sir Christopher Wren and consecrated in 1684. In many ways it's the finest of a group of four similar churches Wren designed on large open sites (the others being St Anne's, Soho, the gloriously-named St Andrew by the Wardrobe, and St Andrew Holborn). Wren's own regard was such that he singled out St James's for description and commendation in his letter 'Upon the Building of National Churches'.

The church is built of red brick with Portland stone dressings, while the interior has galleries on three sides supported by square pillars and the nave a barrel vault supported by Corinthian columns. The font, organ case and reredos are excellent examples of the work of Dutchman Grinling Gibbons, widely regarded as the finest wood carver to work in England. The building was funded by the Earl of St Albans, whose beneficence was recorded by the carving of his arms on the keystone blocks over the doors and on the plaster enrichments of the ceiling (he died in 1684, before the church was consecrated).

The church has been associated with many famous people during its lifetime, including William Blake, who was baptised here in 1757; Leopold Stokowski, choirmaster from 1902 until 1905 (before he became internationally famous); and the poet Robert Graves, who was married here in 1918.

Like many central London churches surrounded by commercial buildings, St James's had a dwindling congregation in the '60s and '70s, and when (in 1980) Donald Reeves was offered the post of rector, the Bishop of London allegedly said: "I

> The church hosts Piccadilly Market (piccadilly-market.co.uk); a food market on Mon-Tue 11am-5pm and an arts & crafts market on Wed-Sat 10am-6pm. There's also an on-site café.

don't mind what you do, just keep it open!" In the last few decades attendance and activity have grown, during which St James's has earned a reputation for being a progressive, liberal and campaigning church (it's also the city's most enterprising).

It has an impressive music programme, with free lunchtime recitals on Mondays, Wednesdays and Fridays, as well as regular paid evening concerts (see sjp.org.uk/evening-concerts.html). The church's Southwood 'secret' Garden was created by Viscount Southwood after World War Two (during which the church was badly damaged) as a garden of remembrance 'to commemorate the courage and fortitude of the people of London', and is a venue for sculpture exhibitions.

Duke of Marlborough

Duchess of Marlborough

MARLBOROUGH HOUSE

Marlborough House is little known and rather unsung, but has much to offer: grand architecture, splendid rooms with classic paintings set in the ceilings, magnificent panelling and ornamental plaster work. The 200-room 'house' is also home to many impressive works of art and has a beautiful, largely original, 18th-century garden.

It was built for Sarah Churchill, Duchess of Marlborough (1660-1744), the favourite confidante and retainer of Queen Anne, who wanted her house to be 'strong, plain, convenient and good'. Christopher Wren, both father and son, designed the brick building with rusticated stone quoins, which was completed in 1711. It was a simple, dignified design, almost plain, and the only bravura was the splendid historical paintings of the Duke's battles which line the walls of the central salon and the staircases. The design was a direct departure from the newly popular Palladian style, a European style of architecture derived from the designs of the Venetian architect Andrea Palladio (1508-1580). The most outstanding and interesting feature was the material used to construct it – Dutch red brick – brought to England as ballast on ships that carried the Duke's troops to Holland.

The house was the London residence of the Dukes of Marlborough for over a century and one of the last private palaces to be built during the reign of Queen Anne (1702-1714). Although not originally a royal residence, it owed its creation to the privileges bestowed by Queen Anne upon the great British military hero, John Churchill, the first Duke of Marlborough (1650-1722), and his wife, Sarah. Along with the dukedom, the royal manor of Woodstock, and a generous financial grant to build the fabulous Blenheim Palace, Queen Anne also granted the Duke and his wife the lease of several acres of land near her London residence, St James's Palace, on which to build a city palace of their own.

On the death of the fourth Duke of Marlborough in 1817, the Crown purchased the lease of Marlborough House, which became the home of assorted royals until the death of the last royal occupant, Queen Mary, in 1953. In 1959, the house was passed to the British Government and since 1965 has been home to the Commonwealth Secretariat, the central body of the Commonwealth of Nations.

For lovers of royal history, Marlborough House has a wealth of physical and sentimental attractions, and although it may not be London's most notable or architecturally-significant royal palace, it has a unique and fascinating character and is well worth a visit.

Address: The Mall, SW1Y 5AH (020-7930 3647, ica.art)

Opening hours: Tue-Thu, Sun noon-11pm, Fri-Sat noon-midnight, closed Mon

Cost: Exhibitions £4, cinema & exhibition peak £13 (off-peak £8); free entry to exhibitions on Tue. Cinema concessions and free exhibition tickets for under 18s, over 65s and various others.

Transport: Charing Cross tube/rail

INSTITUTE OF CONTEMPORARY ARTS

The Institute of Contemporary Arts (ICA) is one of London's leading artistic and cultural centres, containing galleries, a theatre, two cinemas, a good bookshop and a great bar. It's located within Nash House, part of Carlton House Terrace, a grand Regency period building on The Mall – a refreshing hidden gem in a totally unexpected neighbourhood.

The ICA was founded by a group of radical artists in 1946 to challenge the foundations of contemporary art. Its founders wished to establish a space where artists, writers and scientists could debate ideas outside the traditional confines of 'retrograde institutions' such as the Royal Academy. After occupying a variety of 'temporary' locations, the ICA moved to its present splendid abode in 1968, which has become the home of British avant-garde. Originally conceived as a 'laboratory' or 'playground' for contemporary arts, the ICA continues to challenge the traditional notions and boundaries of all forms of art.

In its early years the Institute organised exhibitions of modern art, including Pablo Picasso and Jackson Pollock, and also launched Pop art, Op art, and British Brutalist art and architecture. Contributing to its history have been a who's who of artists and luminaries such as TS Eliot, Stravinsky, Elizabeth Lutyens, Ronnie Scott, Cartier-Bresson, Michel Foucault, Jeff Koons, Peter Blake, Yoko Ono, Don Letts, Wong Kar Wai, Lars von Trier, Takeshi Kitano, Jeff Wall, Vivienne Westwood, Malcolm McClaren, Ian McEwan, Philip Pullman and Zadie Smith – to name just a 'few'. It has also played host to debut solo shows from some of today's highest profile artists including Damien Hirst, Jake & Dinos Chapman, Luc Tuymans and Steve McQueen.

> The cinemas show a brilliant selection of avant-garde and international films, classics and documentaries – perfect if you want to see something other than the usual blockbuster at the local Odeon.

The ICA stages a wide variety of musical acts and was one of the first venues to present The Clash in 1976 and the Stone Roses in 1989, and has seen debut London gigs from many bands that have become household names. It also played host to the first iTunes Festival in 2007 with shows from the likes of Paul McCartney, Amy Winehouse and Kate Nash.

The ICA is never afraid of breaking the rules and doing something different, so expect the unexpected – no one who's serious about contemporary art can afford to ignore it. It's also home to the excellent Rochelle Canteen restaurant and bar.

Address: Horse Guards Parade, Whitehall, SW1A 2AX (020-7930 3070, householdcavalrymuseum.co.uk)

Opening hours: daily 10am-6pm (Apr-Oct), 10am-5pm (Nov-Mar)

Cost: adults £8.50, children (5-16) and concessions £6.50, families (max. 2 adults, 3 children) £22.50

Transport: Charing Cross or Embankment tube

HOUSEHOLD CAVALRY MUSEUM

The Household Cavalry Museum is a unique living museum – about real people doing a real job in a real place. Unlike other military museums, it offers a rare 'behind-the-scenes' look at the ceremonial and operational roles of the Household Cavalry Regiment; you can even see troopers working with horses in the original 18th-century stables through a large glazed partition. The experience is brought to life through personal stories, first-hand accounts of troopers' rigorous and demanding training, interactive displays and rare objects.

The museum sits within Horse Guards in Whitehall in one of the city's most historic buildings, dating from 1750 – the headquarters of the Household Division – where the Household Cavalry performs the daily 'changing of the guard' in a ceremony that has remained broadly unchanged for over 350 years.

The Household Cavalry was formed in 1661 by order of Charles II and consists of the two senior regiments of the British Army: the Life Guards and the Blues and Royals. The cavalry has two roles: as a mounted regiment that guards Her Majesty The Queen on ceremonial occasions in London and across the UK (and is a key part of royal pageantry); and as an operational regiment in the British Army that serves around the world in armoured fighting vehicles (units have been deployed in Iraq and Afghanistan).

Over the centuries the Household Cavalry has amassed an outstanding collection of rare and unique treasures from ceremonial uniforms, royal standards and gallantry awards, to musical instruments, horse furniture and silverware by Fabergé.

Each exhibit has its own story to tell, including two silver kettledrums given to the regiment in 1831 by William IV; the pistol ball that wounded Sir Robert Hill at Waterloo; and the cork leg which belonged to the first Marquess of Anglesey, who lost his leg at Waterloo.

Modern additions to the collection include footballer Jackie Charlton's football cap (he did his national service with the regiment) and the bridle of Sefton, the horse that was injured in the 1982 Hyde Park IRA bombings.

Much of the collection has resulted from the close association between the Household Cavalry and royalty, whom the regiment has protected from rebels, rioters and assassins for over 350 years. The Changing of the Queen's Life Guard takes place daily at 11am on Horse Guards Parade and the daily inspection at 4pm.

The museum shop sells a wide range of gifts and souvenirs.

Address: St Margaret Street, SW1P 3JX (020-7654 4840, westminster-abbey.org/st-margarets-church)

Opening hours: Mon-Fri 9.30am-3.30pm, Sat 9.30am-1.30pm, Sun 2.30-4.30pm. See website for service times.

Cost: free

Transport: Westminster tube

ST MARGARET'S CHURCH

Standing between Westminster Abbey and the Houses of Parliament, it may seem surprising to find another large church. This came about when, in 1065 (just one year before the Norman conquest), Edward the Confessor gave orders for the consecration of the Collegiate Church of St Peter: Westminster Abbey. However, the Benedictine monks of the newly-founded monastery were constantly disturbed by the populace who came to hear mass, so they built a smaller church next to the Abbey where the local people could worship. The church was dedicated to the now little-known St Margaret of Antioch, one of the most popular saints among the laity in medieval England.

The first church was Romanesque in style and survived until the reign of Edward III (1327-77), when the nave was replaced with one in the Perpendicular style. However, towards the end of the 15th century the church had fallen into disrepair and needed almost total reconstruction. Robert Stowell started to rebuild it in 1482, which continued until its consecration in 1523. Despite further restorations in the 18th, 19th and 20th centuries, the structure is still essentially the same; the church's interior was restored and altered by Sir George Gilbert Scott in 1877, although many original Tudor features were retained.

Notable features include the east (Flemish stained glass) window of 1509, which commemorates the betrothal of Catherine of Aragon to Henry VIII. Other windows commemorate William Caxton, England's first printer, buried at the church in 1491; Sir Walter Raleigh, executed in Old Palace Yard and buried here in 1618; the blind poet John Milton, who married here and was a parishioner; and Admiral Robert Blake, responsible for England's naval supremacy in the 17th century. The church is a popular venue for 'society' weddings, including those of Samuel Pepys (1655) and Sir Winston Churchill (1908).

It's thought that St Margaret's was built in the latter part of the 11th century, and until the Dissolution of the Monasteries by Henry VIII in 1540 the monks ministered to the spiritual needs of the people of Westminster. Thus was formed the close relationship between St Margaret's and Westminster Abbey, which has continued to this day.

St Margaret's became the parish church of the Palace of Westminster in 1614, when the Puritans of the 17th century, unhappy with the highly liturgical Abbey, chose to hold Parliamentary services in the more 'suitable' St Margaret's. This practice continues to this day and has led St Margaret's to be dubbed 'the parish church of the House of Commons.'

AT A GLANCE

Address: Abingdon Street, SW1P 3JX (020-7222 2219, english-heritage. org.uk/visit/places/jewel-tower)

Opening hours: summer/autumn 10am-5/6pm, winter/spring, weekends 10am-6pm; see website for exact days and times.

Cost: adults £5.70, concessions £5.10, children £3.40. Free for English Heritage members.

Transport: Westminster tube

JEWEL TOWER

Sitting between the Houses of Parliament and Westminster Abbey, the Jewel Tower (not to be confused with the Jewel House in the Tower of London, which houses the Crown Jewels) is often overlooked. It's appropriately named as this gem of a building is one of only two surviving sections of the medieval royal Palace of Westminster, the other being Westminster Hall. It was built in around 1365 to house the treasures of Edward III, when it was also called the 'King's Privy Wardrobe'. The tower was designed by master mason, Henry Yevele (1320-1400), who was also responsible for the nave of Westminster Abbey and the remodelling of Westminster Hall.

The three-storey building, constructed mainly of Kentish ragstone, was built in an 'L' shaped design in order to fit into a corner of the royal gardens. This forced the builders to encroach onto land belonging to Westminster Abbey, which led to the monks building a new boundary wall (still standing and now part of Westminster School) between the palace and the abbey. The tower was built into the palace's defensive walls and was surrounded by a moat on two sides, the remains of which can still be seen adjacent to the tower.

The tower was detached from the main buildings, which explains its survival when a massive fire in 1834 destroyed most of the remaining palace. In the early 17th century it became a records office for the House of Lords, and from 1869 until 1936 was the home of the Board of Trades Standards Department (evidenced by the display of weights and measuring equipment that you see today).

Today the Jewel Tower is managed by English Heritage and home to the 'Parliament Past and Present' exhibition, which chronicles the evolution of government across the centuries, from the signing of the Magna Carta in the Middle Ages, the testing times of the Reformation and Henry VIII, the violent climax of the Civil War between Charles I and Parliamentary forces, to the present day. Appropriately, the Jewel Tower is a vivid example of how the architecture of Westminster has evolved, from this austere tower to the grandiose Gothic exteriors of today's Palace of Westminster.

> The ground floor of the building retains its superb, original 14th-century ribbed vaulting adorned with 16 unusual bosses of animals, grotesque human faces and green men, which alone merit a visit. A marble table dating from the 13th century is also on display.

Address: **18 Wilton Row, SW1X 7NR (020-7235 3074, grenadierbelgravia. com)**

Opening hours: **Mon-Sat 11am-11.30pm, Sun noon-11.30pm**

Cost: **The price of a drink**

Transport: **Hyde Park Corner or Knightsbridge tube**

THE GRENADIER

The Grenadier is a charming, pocket-sized pub tucked away in an exclusive Belgravia mews, between Hyde Park Corner and Belgrave Square. It's the quintessential picture of an English pub – just as American tourists imagine them – looking more like a misplaced '60s film set than a real pub, in stark contrast to the surrounding grand and very exclusive Belgravia dwellings.

The pub was allegedly built around the Duke of Wellington's officers' mess, but as the area was re-designed in the 1820s (when it was known as Crescent Mews) by Thomas Cubitt, this rather scotches that myth, although it's likely that some of Wellington's troops may have drunk here. Legend has it that the pub's upper floors were once used as the officers' mess of a nearby barracks, while its cellar was pressed into service as a drinking and gambling den for common soldiers.

Nevertheless, the Grenadier is a delightful cosy pub, looking very elegant in its red, white and blue livery, complete with a Victorian gas lamp, original sentry box and flower baskets. Inside, the low coffee-black ceiling, dark panelled walls, original pewter bar and candle-lit ambience give it an air of old-fashioned gentility and timelessness. In keeping with its name, it's packed with military memorabilia, including a genuine busby (bearskin), with the walls covered in military prints, cartoons and press cuttings about the pub, including, not least, its famous resident ghost.

It's said that a young subaltern was caught cheating at cards and suffered such a savage beating by his comrades that he died from his injuries. It's unknown exactly when the incident took place, but it's thought to have occurred in September, as this is when the pub's paranormal activity is at its peak. A number of people have reported seeing a silent sombre spirit gliding across the room before vanishing, and objects are known to disappear or be mysteriously moved overnight. Other phenomena include rattling and moving chairs, footsteps in empty rooms, moaning noises in the cellar, and cold spots reported by patrons and staff (not all reported by inebriated patrons).

> The Grenadier's main claim to fame is its reputation as one of London's most haunted pubs.

The Grenadier has an excellent range of traditional ales on old-fashioned hand pumps and good traditional pub grub served in a small dining area at the back. Your biggest problem will be finding the place – even cabbies struggle – and grabbing a seat; it's best visited during off-peak times.

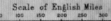

Dr Livingstone's routes between the years 1851 and 1873 ———

ROYAL GEOGRAPHICAL SOCIETY

The Geographical Society of London was founded in 1830 to promote the advancement of geographical science. Like many learned societies at the time, it started life as a dining club, where members held informal debates on current scientific issues and ideas. Under the patronage of William IV, it later became known as the Royal Geographical Society (RGS) and was granted a Royal Charter by Queen Victoria in 1859.

In 1870, the Society found a home at 1 Saville Row – an address that quickly became associated with adventure and travel. In 1913 it moved to its current premises, Lowther Lodge overlooking Hyde Park. The house was built in 1874 for the Hon. William Lowther MP by Richard Norman Shaw (1831-1912), one of the outstanding domestic architects of his day. The lodge (Grade II* listed) is an important example of Victorian Queen Anne architecture. Extensions to the east wing were added in 1929 and included the New Map Room and the 750-seat Lecture Theatre.

The Society's purpose remains the same today as when it was first founded, namely the 'advancement of geographical science'. However, its work has expanded over the years, while continuing to include publishing, supporting field research and expeditions, lectures, conferences and its collections. In its earlier years the Society was closely allied with 'colonial' exploration, particularly in Africa, the Indian subcontinent, the polar regions and central Asia.

The Society is also a pioneer in education and was responsible for introducing the study of geography into schools at the turn of the 20th century. With the advent of a more systematic study of geography, the Institute of British Geographers was formed in 1933 by some Society fellows, and the two organisations co-existed happily until merging in January 1995 (now offcially called the RGS-IBG).

> The Society has been a key associate and supporter of many famous explorers, including Charles Darwin, Sir Edmund Hillary, Henry Cecil John Hunt, David Livingstone, Robert Falcon Scott, Ernest Shackleton and Henry Morton Stanley.

Today the Society has some 15,000 members and Fellows and continues to support and promote geographical research and geography in society. It has a substantial collection of over two million documents, maps, photographs, paintings, periodicals, artefacts and books, spanning 500 years of geography, travel and exploration. The Society organises over 150 events across London each year, many of which are open to the public, including exhibitions in the Pavilion and the Foyle Reading Room.

AT A GLANCE

Address: Lord's Cricket Ground, St John's Wood Road, NW8 8QN (020-7616 8595, lords.org & apps.lords.org/lords/tours-and-museum, tours@lords.org)

Opening hours: The museum can only be visited as part of a tour, which must be booked online. Tours are run seven days a week throughout the year, with the exception of major match days and preparation days (and over Christmas/New Year). Museum access is free for ticket holders on match days. Tours last around 1h 40 mins.

Cost: tours (including museum), adults £25, seniors £20, students £18, under 16s £16

Transport: St John's Wood tube

WG Grace

The Ashes

MCC MUSEUM & TOURS

The Marylebone Cricket Club – usually referred to by its initials 'MCC' – was founded in 1787 and is the world's most famous cricket club. In the 18th century cricket was an exclusive sport played by the gentry and nobility, who, impatient with the crowds who gathered to watch them play, asked Thomas Lord (1755-1832) to establish a new private ground. He leased a ground on Dorset Fields in Marylebone (now Dorset Square), where the first match was staged on 31st May 1787 – and the MCC was born. A year later it laid down a Code of Laws, requiring the wickets to be pitched 22 yards apart and detailing how players could be given out, which were adopted throughout the game. The MCC remains the custodian and arbiter of the laws of cricket to this day.

After a short stay in Marylebone, Lord's – named after the founder of the MCC – moved to a new ground in rural St John's Wood in 1814, which remains the MCC's home to this day. In 1877, the MCC invited Middlesex to adopt Lord's as its county ground, an arrangement which has continued for over 140 years. At the turn of the 20th century the Board of Control for Test Matches and various other bodies were established by the MCC to cater for the growth in domestic and international cricket. Since then the MCC's role has continued to evolve, but it remains the sport's governing body at all levels.

The MCC Museum is the world's oldest sporting museum, housing a wide range of exhibits, although its best-known as the home of 'The Ashes', a tiny terracotta urn reputed to contain the ashes of a burnt cricket bail. After Australia beat

> The Pavilion (1890), restored in 2005, is a listed building and one of the most famous landmarks in world sport. However, a more prominent structure nowadays is the striking futuristic Media Centre – the first all-aluminium, single shell building in the world – which opened for the 1999 Cricket World Cup.

England on an English ground (the Oval) for the first time in 1882, a satirical obituary in The Sporting Times declared that 'English cricket had died and the ashes taken to Australia.' The English media dubbed the next tour to Australia (1882-83) 'the quest to regain The Ashes', during which the urn was presented to the English captain, although it isn't an official trophy. The Museum's extensive collection includes cricket kit used by some of the sport's greatest players – such as Victor Trumper, Jack Hobbs, Don Bradman, Shane Warne and W. G. Grace (probably the most famous cricketer of all time).

AT A GLANCE

Address: 63 Wells Street, W1A 3AE (020-7580 8155, cartoonmuseum.org)

Opening hours: Tue-Sat 10.30am-5.30pm (Thu 8pm), Sun noon-4pm, closed Mon

Cost: adults £8.50, concessions £5, students £3, under 18s free.

Transport: Holborn or Tottenham Court Road tube

CARTOON MUSEUM

The unique Cartoon Museum opened in 2006 and is dedicated to preserving the best of British cartoons, caricatures, comics and animation. The museum allows visitors to enjoy the best of original British cartoon and comic art, from Steve Bell and Matt to Hogarth and Gillray, Giles and Heath Robinson to favourite comic characters such as Andy Capp, Dennis the Menace, the Viz bunch and Roy of the Rovers. Forced to leave its previous home in Little Russell Street, the museum moved to new premises in Fitzrovia in July 2019. The new Cartoon Museum has two large galleries and numerous displays exhibiting original artwork from British comics, graphic novels, newspapers and magazines from the 18th century to the present day.

The main exhibition gallery, curated by the Guardian's Steve Bell, tells the story of the history of cartoon and comic art with examples from the museum's collection of 6,000 pieces. Cartoons are displayed chronologically, starting with the early 18th century, when high-society types back from the Grand Tour introduced the Italian practice of the caricature to polite society. From Hogarth the displays move on to British cartooning's 'golden age' (1770-1830), while 'Modern Times' covers political wartime cartoons and social commentary produced between 1914 and 1961.

A new exhibition explores comic creations that have become imbued in the national consciousness, alongside others who arguably deserve to be. A case in point might be Bunter, the famous stout comic star who first appeared in 1908, who's

> The museum's archives are open to all for the purposes of education, research and enjoyment, and there's also a reference library containing over 5,000 books (on cartoons, comics, caricature and animation) and some 4,000 comics.

displayed next to Hungry Horace, a little-remembered character in Sparky whose love of cakes, sausage rolls, milkshakes and biscuits regularly got him in trouble. Other strips on display include Tinker, a girl's comic character based on Tinkerbell; and Marvelman from the 1950s, perhaps the first successful British superhero. The exhibition is the first of what will be three temporary shows a year at the museum.

The museum's learning programme provides a range of stimulating workshops that encourage young people to explore their creativity and be inspired by the wide variety of cartoons and comic pages in the museum's collection. Workshops are tailored to suit all ages and levels of ability, taught by professional artists and writers with many years teaching experience.

1. Gresham College
2. St Andrew Holborn
3. St Sepulchre-Without-Newgate
4. Museum of London
5. St Dunstan-in-the-West
6. Ye Olde Cheshire Cheese
7. St Mary-Le-Bow
8. Mansion House
9. Royal Exchange
10. Leadenhall Market
11. Bevis Marks Synagogue
12. St Dunstan-in-the-East Garden
13. Temple Church
14. Middle Temple Hall & Gardens
15. Fishmongers' Hall
16. Old Bailey

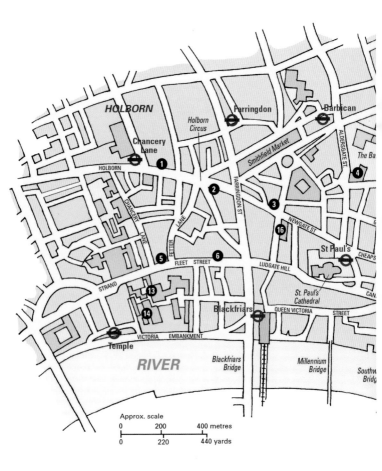

CHAPTER 2

CITY OF LONDON

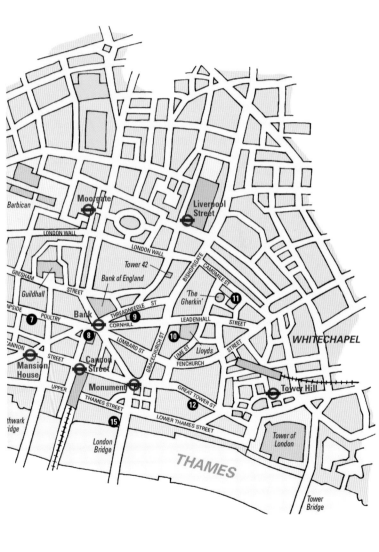

Address: Barnard's Inn Hall, 30 Holborn, EC1N 2HH (020-7831 0575, gresham.ac.uk)

Opening hours: the college isn't open to visitors but anyone can attend the college's free lectures (some require a reservation)

Cost: free

Transport: Chancery Lane tube

Sir Thomas Gresham

GRESHAM COLLEGE

Founded in 1597, Gresham College – named after Sir Thomas Gresham (1519-1579), who built the first Royal Exchange (see page 71) – is London's oldest higher education institution, where professors have given free public lectures for over 400 years.

Gresham's fine mansion in Bishopsgate was the first home of Gresham College, where professors gave their lectures until 1768, their salaries being met from rental income from the shops around the Royal Exchange (which Sir Thomas had bequeathed jointly to the City of London Corporation and the Mercers' Company). This period saw the formation and early development at Gresham College of The Royal Society, and the tenure of chairs by a number of distinguished professors, including Sir Christopher Wren. In later years, lectures were given in various places in the City until the construction of a new Gresham College, opened in 1842, in Gresham Street.

Since 1991, the College has been based at Barnard's Inn Hall, which was part of the estate of Adam de Basing, Mayor of London, in 1252. In 1454 the property was established as an Inn of Chancery (a school for law students), which then passed on to the Inns of Court. Barnard's Inn, together with Staple Inn, became associated with Gray's Inn. In 1892 the freehold was purchased by the Mercers' Company and the building housed the Mercers' School from 1894 until 1959.

In 1985 the Chair of Commerce, funded by the Mercers' School Memorial Trust, was added to the seven ancient Professorships of Astronomy, Divinity, Geometry, Law, Music, Physic and Rhetoric. Professors generally have a three-year tenure. Since 2000, the college

> The hall dates from the late 14th century, with early 16th-century linen-fold panelling. The historic chalk and tile walling preserved in the southern wall of the council chamber below the hall is much older, dating from the Roman period.

has welcomed visiting speakers who deliver lectures on topics outside its usual range, and it also hosts occasional seminars and conferences. Today the college provides over 140 lectures a year, all of which are free and open to the public. It doesn't enrol any students and awards no degrees.

Although some of the lectures are held in Barnard's Inn Hall, the majority take place in the lecture hall at the Museum of London (see page 61) for reasons of capacity. A programme of lectures can be viewed on the college's website.

ST ANDREW HOLBORN

This Grade I listed church sits on a Roman site and has a long and interesting history. St Andrew Holborn (named St Andrew Holburnestrate/St Andrew de Holeburn in the Middle Ages) first appears in written records in AD951 as a church on top of the hill above the River Fleet. However, excavation of the crypt in 2002 discovered Roman pottery, indicating the site has been in use for much longer. In 1348, a local armourer, John Thavie, 'left a considerable estate towards the support of the fabric forever', and it's his legacy – preserved during the Reformation and carefully invested through the centuries – that still provides for the upkeep of the church today.

The original wooden church was replaced by a stone building in the 15th century, of which only the tower now remains. From the outside the tower looks like it was built by Sir Christopher Wren, but inside you can see its medieval masonry. During the Great Fire of 1666, the church was saved at the 11th hour by a change in the wind direction. However, as it was in a bad state of repair it was rebuilt by Wren, who clad the tower in marble, leaving the crypt, which still exists beneath the church.

The church is the final resting place of Thomas Coram (1668-1751), who founded the Foundling Hospital in 1741, and was also the founding place of the Royal Free Hospital, after William Marsden (1796-1867) found a dying girl in the churchyard in 1827, which inspired him to establish a hospital in Greville Street for the poor and destitute. As part of the Holborn improvement scheme in the mid-19th century, the church lost its north churchyard, but used the compensation to build a new vicarage and Court House (designed by Samuel Teulon) on the south side of the church.

> St Andrew Holborn stands as a monument to Wren and the many master craftsmen who brought this magnificent church back to life.

Teulon's alterations were destroyed when the church was bombed and gutted by fire in 1941, leaving only the exterior walls and tower of the original building. After much delay, it was decided that the church would be restored 'stone for stone and brick for brick' to the original Wren design. The present building opened in 1961 with the new status of Guild Church, i.e. a church without a parish designed to serve the local working community.

Address: Holborn Viaduct, EC1A 2DQ (020-7236 1145, hsl.church)

Opening hours: opening hours vary (telephone or contact office@hsl.church); see website for service times, concerts and recitals

Cost: free

Transport: Farringdon or St Paul's tube

Execution Bell

ST SEPULCHRE-WITHOUT-NEWGATE

St Sepulchre-without-Newgate, aka the Church of the Holy Sepulchre, is the largest parish church in the City of London with a fascinating history dating back to 1137, when it was given to the Priory of St Bartholomew. The churchyard dates from around 1240 and a cross is mentioned in the south churchyard in 1370. The church was rebuilt in the 15th century by Sir Hugh Popham, Treasurer of the King's Household and Chancellor of Normandy. After the Dissolution of the Monasteries it remained in the possession of the Crown until 1610.

Much of the present building dates from 1670 when Sir Christopher Wren rebuilt the earlier structure largely destroyed in the Great Fire, although by 1790 it was in a state of decay and was substantially restored. Part of the former churchyard is now a public garden to the south and east of the church, which incorporates a Garden of Remembrance to soldiers of the Royal Fusiliers City of London Regiment (there's also a chapel dedicated to them), which has historical connections with the church. The church is the final resting place of Captain John Smith (1580-1631), first Governor of Virginia, USA.

Nowadays St Sepulchre's is best known as the National Musicians' Church, with a beautiful chapel dedicated to musicians. The School of English Church Music (now the Royal School of Church Music) had its first London base at St Sepulchre's and was used regularly for BBC broadcasts in the

> Displayed in the church is the Execution Bell (left), a grim reminder of the church's connection with the old Newgate Prison which, until 1902, stood on the site now occupied by the Central Criminal Court (The Old Bailey). In 1605, Robert Dowe gave £50 for the ringing of the great bell on the mornings of executions, and for other services concerning condemned prisoners, including the ringing of the bell at midnight outside the condemned cell by the bellman of St Sepulchre.

1930s. The young Henry Wood – who founded the Promenade Concerts at the Royal Albert Hall – learnt to play the organ in the St Stephen Harding Chapel and was appointed assistant organist at the age of 14. When he died in 1944 his ashes were laid to rest in the chapel, which was subsequently renamed the Musicians' Chapel.

St Sepulchre's has a thriving musical tradition – with links to many music colleges and institutions – and provides an important venue for musical events and a centre for musicians. It's one of the City's best places to take in a concert or recital.

MUSEUM OF LONDON

Not exactly hidden, but being isolated in the City the Museum of London isn't as widely known as it merits. It's vast – the largest urban history museum in the world – and primarily concerned with the social history of London and its inhabitants throughout history. It documents the city's history from the prehistoric to the present day, and is operated as a social and urban history museum, but maintains its archaeological interests. There are a number of permanent galleries, including: London before London; Roman London; Medieval London Gallery; War, Fire and Plague (covering the English Civil War, the Plague and the Great Fire of London); and galleries for the periods 1666-1850s (Expanding City); 1850s-1940s (People's City); and the 1950s to today (World City); and 'The City Gallery'. The museum opened a sister museum – the Museum of London Docklands – in 2003.

The City Gallery celebrates the City of London itself, through displays that showcase the area's unique character, a place where ancient traditions exist alongside cutting edge architecture. Its centrepiece is the magnificent Lord Mayor's Coach, now over 250 years old, commissioned in 1757 for the Lord Mayor's Show and still used every November. The Sackler Hall is a large, contemporary hub that forms the heart of the Museum and provides a space for rest and refreshment.

The Museum of London is an amalgamation of two earlier museums: the Guildhall Museum, founded in 1826, and the London Museum, founded in 1912. The Guildhall Museum was largely archaeological, its first acquisition being a fragment of Roman mosaic, while the London Museum had wider interests, collecting modern objects, paintings and costumes, alongside archaeology. Both collections came together after World War Two and the new Museum of London opened in 1976. The architects were Philip Powell and Hidalgo Moya, who adopted an innovative approach to museum design, whereby the galleries were laid out so that there was only one route through the museum, from the prehistoric period to the modern galleries.

> In 2016 the museum announced plans to move half a mile to the west to the historic Smithfield Market site, which is expected to take place in around 2025 (see museum.london).

There's a changing programme of exhibitions showcasing creative talent in London, and regular free gallery tours. There's also a programme of courses and talks relating to London's history and archaeology for adults of all ages and interests.

The museum also has two cafés and an excellent bookshop.

Address: 186a Fleet Street, EC4A 2HR (020-7405 1929, stdunstaninthewest.org)

Opening hours: Mon-Fri 10am-4pm, music recitals Wed & Fri 1.15pm (see website for dates and services times)

Cost: free

Transport: Chancery or Temple tube

ST DUNSTAN-IN-THE-WEST

The church of St Dunstan-in-the-West has a long and illustrious history, the original church being built between 988 and 1070AD. Dunstan (909-988), one of the foremost Saints of Anglo-Saxon England, was taught by Irish monks at Glastonbury Abbey (Somerset), where he was later adopted as the patron Saint of Goldsmiths. He became a companion to King Aethelstan's stepbrothers, Edmund and Eadred, although he was banished after the king died in 939. He was appointed abbot of Glastonbury in 945 and later Bishop of Worcester and then Bishop of London, before becoming Archbishop of Canterbury in 960 (he's buried in the cathedral). He died in 988 on 19th May, his feast day, and was the most popular saint in England for almost two centuries, until being overshadowed by Thomas Becket's fame in the 12th century.

St Dunstan's narrowly escaped the Great Fire in 1666, thanks to the quick thinking of the Dean of Westminster, who roused scholars from Westminster School to extinguish the flames. But wear and tear took its toll and St Dunstan's was rebuilt in 1831 by architect John Shaw and his son. The tower was badly damaged during World War Two and was rebuilt in 1950. In 1952, St Dunstan's became a Guild Church, dedicated to the daytime working population around Fleet Street, and in 2003 was designated the Diocese of London's 'Church for Europe'.

The church was a well-known landmark in previous centuries thanks to its magnificent clock – which dates from 1671 – the first public clock in London with a minute hand. The figures of the two giants, Gog and Magog, strike the hours and quarters, and turn their heads. The courtyard also contains statues of King Lud, the mythical sovereign, and his sons, and Elizabeth I, which dates from 1586 and is the only statue of her known to have been carved during her reign (and the only statue with its own income, thanks to a bequest in 1929). Much of the internal fabric pre-dates the rebuilding of the church in the 1830s. The high altar and reredos are Flemish woodwork dating from the 17th century and there are two bronze figures thought to date from 1530.

> St Dunstan's is the only church in Britain to possess a chapel or shrine to seven different churches of Christendom, including a Romanian Orthodox chapel.

St Dunstan's is noted for its free lunchtime classical music recitals on selected Wednesdays and Fridays (1.15pm), which provide an opportunity for a relaxing break.

Address: Wine Office Court, 145 Fleet Street, EC4A 2BU (020-7353 6170)
Opening hours: Mon-Sat 11am-11pm, closed Sun
Cost: the price of a drink
Transport: Blackfriars tube or City Thameslink rail

YE OLDE CHESHIRE CHEESE

Ye Olde Cheshire Cheese is one of the oldest pubs in the City, dating to 1667 during the reign of Charles II, the previous one having been destroyed in the Great Fire in 1666. But there's been a pub on this site since at least 1538, when the Horn Tavern is recorded. It's one of the City's most atmospheric pubs, thanks to its lack of natural lighting, (possibly original) wood panelling and cellar-like rooms. The vaulted cellars are thought to have belonged to a 13th-century Carmelite Monastery which once occupied the site. The unassuming entrance in a narrow alleyway belies the ample space and number of bars and rooms within, while in winter an open fire provides warmth and atmosphere.

In the bar room are posted plaques showing famous people who were regulars or visitors. From the 1850s the Cheese was on the itinerary of many visitors to London and over the centuries has attracted many distinguished drinkers, including such literary luminaries as Oliver Goldsmith, Alfred Tennyson, Mark Twain, Sir Arthur Conan Doyle, G. K. Chesterton, Ben Jonson, Edward Gibbon, Thomas Carlyle, James Boswell and Dr Samuel Johnson (who lived in Gough Square nearby). Charles Dickens was known to frequent the Cheese and may well have modelled some of his characters on regulars here (the pub is alluded to in *A Tale of Two Cities*). The Rhymers' Club, a group of London-based poets, founded in 1890 by W. B. Yeats and Ernest Rhys, also used to meet here.

Approached through a narrow alleyway (Wine Office Court), the Cheese beckons you into a bygone age; next to the entrance is a notice board listing reigning monarchs during the pub's over 350-year existence. Today the pub is operated by Yorkshire's Samuel Smith brewery, which has a reputation for excellent 'real' ales. The atmosphere is warm and friendly (if dark), with a multitude of rooms, stairs, nooks & crannies. There's a chop room on the ground floor, so you can enjoy both the surroundings and good traditional food – without the distractions of muzak, widescreen TV or pub quizzes.

By 1900, the Cheese had a resident 'who' was to become almost as famous as the pub itself – Polly the eccentric parrot. Polly was famous far and wide for her antics, intelligence and ability to mime – and her rudeness to patrons! When she died in 1926, she was thought to be aged over 40 and her obituary appeared in over 200 newspapers.

AT A GLANCE

Address: Cheapside, EC2V 6AU (020-7248 5139, stmarylebow.co.uk)

Opening hours: Mon-Wed 7.30am-6pm, Thu until 6.30pm, Fri 4pm. See website for service times.

Cost: free

Transport: Bank, Mansion House or St Paul's tube

ST MARY-LE-BOW

Like many City churches, St Mary-le-Bow is often overlooked, but has a long and varied history. It was built around 1080 by Lanfranc (1005-1089), William the Conqueror's Archbishop of Canterbury (who accompanied him from Bec in Normandy), as his London HQ. It's thought that Gundulf, Bishop of Rochester, was the architect. The Norman church, which possibly replaced a building of Saxon origin, was constructed from the same Caen stone as the Tower of London. The church survived three devastating collapses before being destroyed in the Great Fire of 1666. Rebuilt by Sir Christopher Wren, it was destroyed once more in World War Two but was again rebuilt and re-consecrated in 1964.

The crypt which sits beneath the 11th-century church was the first arched crypt found in any church in London. The 'le-Bow' in the church's name derives from these arches, the importance of which is attested to by its Latin name, *Sancta Marie-de-Arcubus*. Of that interior, no reliable image (before the Great Fire) survives. From around 1251, St Mary's was home to the final appeal court of the southern province of the church, and would have been alive to the buzz of clergy and canon lawyers. It remains the meeting place of the Court of Arches, the final appeal court of the Canterbury province, and is also where most English bishops receive confirmation of their election.

Today St Mary-le-Bow is probably best known as the church of 'Bow bells' and it's said that only those born within earshot of its bells are entitled to call themselves true Cockneys. The curfew bell that rang at St Mary from

> It was allegedly on hearing Bow's bells that Richard (Dick) Whittington returned to London in the 14th century to seek his fortune and become Lord Mayor (four times!).

1472 wasn't used just to mark the end of the working day, but was also part of the daily routines of prayer.

After the Great Fire, St Mary's was rebuilt by Sir Christopher Wren between 1671-80 – based on the Temple of Peace in Rome – and it's often cited as the most distinguished of his City churches.

Nowadays St Mary-le-Bow is something of an anomaly – a parish without residents or Sunday services – although it remains an active church serving all who work in and visit the City. The Academy of St Mary-le-Bow was formed in 2016 and the church holds regular concerts and recitals, including free lunchtime recitals (1.05pm) – see website for information. There's also an excellent café (Café Below, 020-7329 0789) in the crypt, serving breakfast and lunch Mon-Fri.

AT A GLANCE

Address: Walbrook, EC4N 8BH (020-7626 2500, cityoflondon.gov.uk/about-the-city/mansion-house)

Opening hours: Guided tours (1 hour) Tue 2pm – to book, see eventbrite.co.uk/e/tour-of-the-mansion-house-tickets-65160817760?aff=erelexpml.

Cost: tours £9.50 adults, £7.50 concessions; group tours can also be arranged.

Transport: Bank tube

MANSION HOUSE

The Mansion House is a City gem – a rare surviving grand Georgian town palace – which you can visit. It's the official residence of the Lord Mayor of the City of London, the Lord Mayor's private office, a department of the City of London Corporation, and provides a centre for business meetings, conferences, banquets and entertaining. (The Lord Mayor is elected for one year, the position being unpaid and apolitical, not to be confused with the Mayor of London, which is a paid, elected, political position with a four-year term.)

Mansion House has magnificent interiors and elegant furniture, and is used for a number of the City's grandest official functions, including an annual dinner hosted by the Lord Mayor, at which the Chancellor of the Exchequer gives his 'Mansion House Speech' regarding the state of the British economy. It was built between 1739 and 1752 by the architect and Clerk of the City's Works, George Dance the Elder; the site had formerly been occupied by St Mary Woolchurch Haw church, which was destroyed in the Great Fire (1666).

Mansion House's design is a classical Palladian style with ornate gold trim, Corinthian columns and a grand Egyptian Hall (seating 350) on the first floor. The hall isn't, however, Egyptian in style, but is based on designs by the classical Roman architect Vitruvius of Roman buildings in Egypt, with giant columns supporting a narrower attic area. The second floor contains a ballroom and the private apartments of the Lord Mayor. The building has played host to many momentous occasions of global importance over the last two and a half centuries.

Mansion House is home to a magnificent collection of gold and silver plate – one

> The cellars once held prisoners' cells, due to the building's former use as the Lord Mayor's Court. The famous suffragette Emmeline Pankhurst, campaigner for women's rights, was once held prisoner here.

of the best in the world and still in use on ceremonial occasions – a collection of sculptures, and one of the finest art collections outside London's public art galleries. This includes the Harold Samuel Art Collection of eighty-four 17th-century Dutch and Flemish paintings by masters such as Frans Hals, Nicolaes Maes, Jacob van Ruisdael and Jan Steen (bequeathed to the City in 1987). It's probably the best collection of Dutch art in Britain and adds further splendour to the Mansion House's interior.

Address: Threadneedle Street, EC3V 3LR (020-7409 8875, theroyalexchange.co.uk)

Opening hours: Mon-Fri, shops ca. 10am-6/6.30pm, restaurants 8am-11pm

Cost: free

Transport: Bank tube

ROYAL EXCHANGE

The Grade I listed Royal Exchange (RE) is a building steeped in history, although often overlooked in favour of its more illustrious neighbours. From its proud beginnings in 1565 to its latest incarnation as a luxury shopping centre, the RE has always stood for trade. Today, flanked by the Mansion House, the Bank of England and close to the Lloyd's building, the Royal Exchange sits at the heart of London's commercial hub.

Early 16th-century London was fuelled by commerce, with merchants coming from throughout Europe to trade their wares, negotiating in shops, homes, taverns and even in the streets. Meanwhile in the great port of Antwerp, merchants had a base within which to trade – a Bourse – where trade was regulated and controlled, and credit could be guaranteed and loans raised. Richard Gresham, a London cloth merchant (who supplied the tapestries for Henry VIII's Hampton Court), realised the trading centre's importance and urged the establishment of a similar centre in London. However, it was to fall to his son, Thomas, to realise his father's vision. (See also **Gresham College** on page 55.)

The first Royal Exchange was established in 1565 but wasn't officially opened (by Elizabeth I) until 1571. The resulting building, adorned with the Gresham family crest of a grasshopper (which can still be

> The Royal Exchange survived World War Two and was used variously by a theatre company, the Guardian Royal Exchange (GRE) and (in 1982) by the London International Financial Futures Exchange (LIFFE). It was restored in the '80s, when 20 new Corinthian capitals were installed. After refurbishment in 2001 it became a luxury shopping centre and a showplace for many of Britain's and the world's finest merchants and a number of excellent restaurants.

seen on the weathervane), was to survive until 1666, when it was destroyed in the Great Fire. A second exchange was designed by Edward Jarman and opened in 1669, but was also gutted by fire (in 1838). The third Royal Exchange building, which still stands today, was designed by Sir William Tite and opened by Queen Victoria in 1844. It adheres to the original layout of a four-sided structure surrounding a central courtyard, where merchants and tradesmen could do business. In 1892, 24 large panel paintings were installed on the walls of the ambulatory and can be viewed today. The first, showing Phoenicians trading with ancient Britons on the coast of Cornwall, is by Sir Frederic Leighton (1830-1896); together the paintings constitute a colourful history of British trade from its earliest times.

AT A GLANCE

Address: Gracechurch Street, EC3V 1LT (020-7606 3030, leadenhallmarket.co.uk)

Opening hours: Stalls and shops are open Mon-Fri ca. 9am-7pm, while public areas have unrestricted access

Cost: free

Transport: Bank or Monument tube

LEADENHALL MARKET

Leadenhall Market is an ornate restored Victorian covered market selling traditional game, poultry, fish, meat and 'designer' items, standing on the site of 1st-century Londinium's Roman basilica. In 1411, the site was acquired by Richard 'Dick' Whittington, the Lord Mayor of London, and grew in importance as a granary and chapel were built. In 1463, the beam for the tronage (toll or duty) and weighing of wool was fixed at Leadenhall Market, signifying its importance as a centre for commerce. In 1488, leather was sold exclusively from Leadenhall and cutlery was added in 1622. The market was largely destroyed in the Great Fire (1666) and was rebuilt as a covered structure, when it was divided into a Beef Market, Green Yard and Herb Market. Somewhat surprisingly, in the mid-18th century the porters were women.

The 17th-century building was demolished in 1881 and redesigned by Sir Horace Jones (architect of Billingsgate and Smithfield Markets), when the beautiful ornate wrought iron and glass building (painted green, maroon and cream) you see today was erected (Grade II listed). In 1990-91 it received a dramatic redecoration which transformed its appearance, enhancing the architectural character and detail. The main double height entrance is on Gracechurch Street, flanked by tall, narrow, gabled red brick and Portland stone blocks in a Dutch 17th-century style. The adjacent buildings to the south have a continuous retail frontage, punctuated by narrow entrances to pedestrian alleyways into the market. (It has featured in a number of films – in 2001 it featured as Diagon Alley in *Harry Potter and the Philosopher's Stone*.)

A celebrated 'character' in Leadenhall during the 18th century was 'Old Tom', a goose which managed to escape execution even though it's recorded that 34,000 geese were slaughtered here in two days. He became a great favourite in the market and was fed at local inns. After his death in 1835 at the age of 38, he lay in state in the market and was buried there.

Leadenhall Market sells some of the finest food in the City, including fresh meat and cheese and delicacies from around the world, and has a variety of vendors including a florist, a cigar store, a pen shop and fashion shops, plus a number of restaurants, pubs (try the Lamb Tavern) and wine bars. Leadenhall isn't just a scenic market place but also a lovely place to stroll around; a varied programme of events means the area is always bustling.

Address: Bevis Marks, EC3A 7LH (020-7626 1274, bevismarks.org.uk)

Opening hours: Mon, Wed, Thu, 10.30am-2pm; Tue, Fri, 10.30am-1pm; Sun 10.30am-12.30pm. Closed Sat, Jewish festivals, Tish Be'Av and bank holidays. Conducted tours, Wed, Fri 11.30am, Sun 11am. See website for service times.

Cost: adults £5, seniors £4, children £2.50.

Transport: Aldgate or Liverpool Street tube

BEVIS MARKS SYNAGOGUE

B evis Marks Synagogue is a Grade I listed building and the flagship synagogue of Anglo-Jewry. It's still in regular use as a place of worship and the only synagogue in Europe that has held continuous services for over 300 years.

London's modern Jewish community began with the famous petition presented to Cromwell in 1656 by Rabbi Menasseh Ben Israel of Holland, who was living in London. For the first time since the expulsion in 1290 under Edward I, Jews were permitted to live and worship openly in England. The Jews of London (mostly Spanish and Portuguese) quickly established a synagogue in Creechurch Lane in the City; the community grew steadily and eventually decided to build a large synagogue, Bevis Marks, completed in 1701. The interior is modelled on the great Amsterdam synagogue of 1677, while the roof incorporates a beam from a royal ship presented by Queen Anne.

The roof was destroyed by fire in 1738 and repaired in 1749, but the remainder of the synagogue remains largely as it was over 300 years ago. In 1992-1993, the Synagogue suffered extensive damage from terrorist bomb attacks, but was quickly repaired and restored to its former glory.

Bevis Marks was the religious centre of the Anglo-Jewish world for over a century and served as a clearing-house for congregational and individual troubles the world over. These included the appeal by Jamaican Jews for a reduction in taxation (1736); the internecine quarrel among the Barbados Jews (1753); and the aiding of seven-year-old Moses de Paz, who escaped from Gibraltar in 1777 to avoid an enforced conversion.

The synagogue's most prominent feature is its beautiful Renaissance-style ark (containing the Torah scrolls) situated at the centre of the eastern wall of the building. Both in its location and design, it's like the reredos of the churches of the same period. Painted to look like coloured Italian marble, it's in fact made entirely of oak. Seven hanging brass candelabra symbolise the seven days of the week, the largest of which represents the Sabbath.

Twelve pillars, symbolising the twelve tribes of Israel, support the women's gallery, while the backless benches at the rear of the synagogue – dating from 1657 – are from the original synagogue at Creechurch Lane and are still in regular use.

ST DUNSTAN-IN-THE-EAST GARDEN

This beautiful garden was one of the author's most delightful discoveries. There has been a church here from ancient times and a large churchyard from the 12th century. In 1366, St Dunstan-in-the-East required rebuilding (when the Archbishop forced parishioners to contribute to the cost!) and in 1417 it closed temporarily after a fatal brawl. It was severely damaged in the Great Fire of 1666, but rather than being completely rebuilt it was patched up and a tower and steeple added in 1695-1701 by Sir Christopher Wren. It was built in a Gothic style sympathetic to the main body of the church, although with heavy string courses of a kind unknown in the Middle Ages. The restored church had wooden carvings by Grinling Gibbons and an organ by Father Smith (moved to the abbey at St Albans in 1818 when the church was rebuilt).

The Corporation of London acquired the Grade I listed ruins (the walls, gates and railings are from the Wren period) in 1967, which along with the former churchyard were incorporated into a garden, opened in 1971. It includes a lawn, a circular cobbled area and a low fountain in the middle (what was the nave), lots of benches, unusual trees, shrubs, flowers and climbers growing among the ruined arches and tracery.

Today St Dunstan's is one of the City's most beautiful gardens and a welcome retreat from the surrounding bustle. Visitors can enjoy a huge variety of plants wending their way around the ruins; the walls and

> St Dunstan's was largely destroyed in the blitz of 1941 – only the north and south walls remained – although Wren's tower and steeple survived intact. The spire was reconstructed in 1953 and the tower restored in 1970-1, but it was decided not to rebuild the church. The tower and adjoining All Hallows House have been converted to residential use.

majestic windows have been draped and decorated with Virginia creeper and ornamental vine, which turn crimson in autumn. Exotic plants such as pineapple-scented Moroccan broom and New Zealand flax thrive in the sheltered conditions, while in the lower garden is winter's bark (with leaves high in vitamin C, once eaten to prevent scurvy), and a Japanese snowball by the fountain that displays breathtaking blossom in late spring.

Occasional services are held in the garden, such as on Palm Sunday before a procession to All Hallows along St Dunstan's Hill and Great Tower Street.

Address: Temple, EC4Y 7BB (020-7353 3470, templechurch.com)

Opening hours: Mon-Fri 10am-4pm, but check as it may be closed for a special service/event (tel or contact verger@templechurch.com). See website for service times.

Cost: £5, £3 seniors & students, under 16s free

Transport: Temple or Chancery Lane tube

TEMPLE CHURCH

At the heart of legal London sits Temple Church, a mysterious, spiritual space with wonderful acoustics, where you can hear some of the City's finest church music. It's also one of London's most striking and historic churches, with 800 years of unbroken history. From the Crusaders in the 12th century, through the turmoil of the Reformation, the Civil War, the Great Fire and World War Two bombs – it has survived virtually intact.

The church is in two parts: the rare circular 'Round' from 1185 and the Chancel (the 'Oblong'), dating from 1240. The Round Church, made of Caen stone, is one of only four Norman round churches remaining in England and was consecrated by Heraclius, Crusader Patriarch of Jerusalem, designed to emulate the holiest place in the Crusaders' world: the Church of the Holy Sepulchre in Jerusalem. Its choir is said to be perfection, with stunning stained glass windows, an impressive organ and a handsome wooden altar by Sir Christopher Wren. Inside the Round Church are nine knightly effigies, which were believed to be tombs until restoration revealed no bodies.

The church was built by the Knights Templar or Red Knights (after the red crosses they wore), the order of crusading monks founded to protect pilgrims travelling to and from Jerusalem in the 12th century. It was originally part of a centre that included residences, military training facilities, and recreational grounds for the military brethren and novices, forbidden to go into the City without permission from the Master of the Temple. The order of the Knights Templar was very powerful in England during this early period – not even answerable to kings – when

> The church was featured in the novel, *The Da Vinci Code*, by Dan Brown, and was also used as a location in the film of the book.

the Master of the Temple sat in Parliament as *primus baro* (the first baron of the realm). After the destruction and abolition of the Knights Templar in 1307, Edward II took control of the church as a crown possession, and it was later given to the Knights Hospitaller (or Knights of Malta).

The church was rented to two colleges of lawyers which evolved into the Inner and Middle Temples, two of the four Inns of Court. Today the Temple Church is held in common by both Inns and is the main chapel of those who work in the Temple, but don't let that deter you from visiting this Gothic-Romanesque masterpiece.

AT A GLANCE

Address: Middle Temple Lane, EC4Y 9AT (020-7427 4800, middletemple.org.uk)

Opening hours: Gardens, weekdays noon-3pm, May-July and September. Tours (minimum of ten people) must be pre-booked, as can lunch (£25/£30) in Middle Temple Hall (020-7427 4820, events@middletemple.org.uk).

Cost: tours £8 per person; entrance to the gardens is free

Transport: Temple tube

MIDDLE TEMPLE HALL & GARDENS

The lovely Middle Temple Hall is probably the finest example of an Elizabethan hall in the UK. It was built between 1562 and 1573 and remains virtually unchanged to this day, having survived the Great Fire and World War Two. Measuring 101 x 41 feet, it's spanned by a magnificent double hammer beam roof carved from the oaks of Windsor Forest, with an elaborately carved screen made in 1574. The traditional oak panelled walls are festooned with coats of arms and the impressive windows are made from heraldic glass memorials to notable barristers from Middle Temple. The 29ft bench table is believed to be a gift from Elizabeth I. The hall remains the centre of life for the Inn today, as bench, bar and students meet here daily for lunch (you can also have lunch in these impressive surroundings).

The Honourable Society of the Middle Temple is one of the four Inns of Court with the exclusive right to call men and women to the Bar (HRH Prince William of Wales – an honorary barrister – was called to the Bench on 6th July 2009, in the Hall.) The Inn is composed of student, barrister and bench members, and is governed by the Masters of the Bench, who are usually senior members of the judiciary or Queen's Counsel.

Although the exact date is unknown, it's believed that the Middle Temple was established by the mid-14th century. The Inn's name derives from the Knights Templar who owned the Temple site for some 150 years. The origins of the Inn can be traced from two roots: the occupation of the Knights Templar and the replacement of the priestly lawyers by a lay profession.

The award-winning gardens of Middle Temple Hall (the best gardens of all four Inns of Court) overlook the River Thames and offer a peaceful haven from the bustle of central London.

> The first performance of Shakespeare's *Twelfth Night* is recorded as having taken place in Middle Temple Hall in 1602.

The gardens may date back to when the Knights Templar first arrived in the 12th century, although today's gardens (and buildings) were reworked in the mid- to late-17th century, when they were enclosed by a brick wall to protect them from flooding. The fountain in Fountain Court is reputedly the oldest permanent fountain in London. The main garden you see today is little changed from the 1870s when Victoria Embankment was constructed and doubled the size of the garden.

See also **Temple Church** on page 79.

FISHMONGERS' HALL

The Fishmongers' Hall is a striking Grade I listed building, enjoying a prime riverside position on the north bank of the Thames at London Bridge. It was destroyed in the Great Fire in 1666, rebuilt twice thereafter, devastated again during World War Two and restored to its former glory by 1954. Its stunning interior is used today as a venue for meetings and banquets and is well worth a visit.

The Worshipful Company of Fishmongers is one of the most ancient of the original Twelve Great Livery Companies of the City of London (it ranks fourth in order of precedence) with a fascinating history. It was established by royal charter from Edward I around 1272, although the Fishmongers of London were recognised as an organised community long before then. The charter (and other later charters) declared that no fish could be sold in London except by the 'Mistery of Fishmongers' ('mistery' is a corruption of the French *métier*, meaning trade).

With a complete monopoly on the sale of fish, one of the chief necessities of life in the Middle Ages, the Company's wealth and influence grew rapidly. Fish was an important part of the Christian diet, as it was forbidden to eat meat on Fridays, holy days and regular fast days, which were most Saturdays and Wednesdays. Eggs and dairy foods were also forbidden during the period of Lent. These restrictions meant that for around half the year people had to eat fish to get a nutritious meal, which made fishmongers a vital part of everyday life and the economy.

As well as playing a prominent part in the affairs of the city, the Company had its own Court of Law (Leyhalmode), where disputes relating to fish were settled. Although the Company gradually lost its monopoly on buying and

> London's most famous fishmonger was Sir William Walworth (d 1385) who, as Lord Mayor of the City of London, ended the Peasants' Revolt in 1381 by stabbing the rebel Wat Tyler to death at Smithfield in the presence of Richard II.

selling fish in the 15th century, it's one of the few ancient livery companies that's still intimately linked to its historic trade.

Fishmongers are also the organisers of the UK's, and probably the world's, oldest sporting event with the longest continuous history, first contested in 1715. The Doggett's Coat and Badge Race (named after its founder, Thomas Doggett, 1640-1721), is an annual sculling race from London Bridge to Chelsea for members of the Company of Watermen and Lightermen.

AT A GLANCE

Address: The Old Bailey, London EC4M 7EH (020-7192 2739, oldbaileyonline.org and courttribunalfinder.service.gov.uk/courts/central-criminal-court)

Opening hours: Mon-Fri 9.30am-3.30pm

Cost: free, tours £12 per head (see old-bailey.com, info@oldbaileyinsight.co.uk)

Transport: St Paul's tube

Lady Justice

OLD BAILEY

Commonly called the Old Bailey after the street on which it stands, the OB is officially the Central Criminal Court of England and Wales, and is one of a number of buildings housing the Crown Court. The Crown Court sitting at the Central Criminal Court deals with major criminal cases in Greater London and, in exceptional cases, from other parts of England and Wales. The court originated as a sessions house of the Lord Mayor and Sheriffs of the City of London, first mentioned in 1585. Located next to the old Newgate Prison, the court was destroyed in the Great Fire of London in 1666 and rebuilt in 1674. In 1834 it was renamed the Central Criminal Court and its jurisdiction extended (beyond London and Middlesex) to the whole of England for trials of major cases.

The Old Bailey has been housed in several structures since the 16th century. The current building – on the site of Newgate Prison – dates from 1902 and was designed in neo-Baroque style by Edward William Mountford (officially opened in 1907 by Edward VII). On the dome above the court stands the famous 12ft bronze statue by F. W. Pomeroy of Lady Justice (see opposite), who holds a sword in her right hand and the scales of justice in her left.

The interior of the Great Hall (beneath the dome) has a monumental staircase, Sicilian marble floors and ornate mosaic arches, and is decorated with allegorical paintings commemorating the World War Two blitz (in which the building was severely damaged), as well as

> The Old Bailey is located adjacent to the infamous medieval Newgate gaol, where until 1868 hangings were a public spectacle. The condemned were led along Dead Man's Walk between the prison and the court, where large crowds would pelt them with rotten fruit and vegetables and stones.

quasi-historical scenes of St Paul's Cathedral. The Great Hall (and the floor beneath it) is decorated with busts and statues, chiefly of British monarchs, but also of legal figures and those who achieved renown by campaigning for improvement in prison conditions in the 18th and 19th centuries. The lower level hosts an exhibition on the fascinating history of the Old Bailey and Newgate, featuring historical prison artefacts.

Trials at the Old Bailey, as at other courts, are open to the public; however, they're subject to stringent security procedures. The public are welcome to visit the splendid historic building and can join a tour.

1. Brompton Oratory
2. Michelin House
3. Saatchi Gallery
4. St Luke's & Garden
5. Brompton Cemetery
6. Cheyne Walk
7. Albert Bridge
8. Design Museum

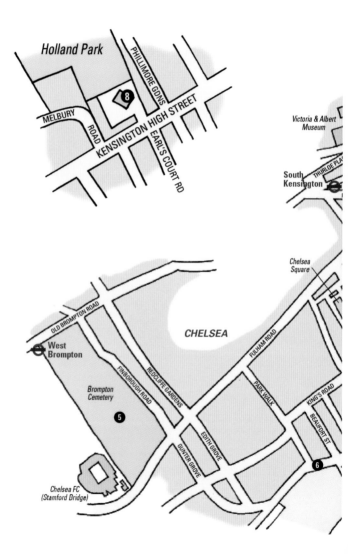

CHAPTER 3

KENSINGTON & CHELSEA

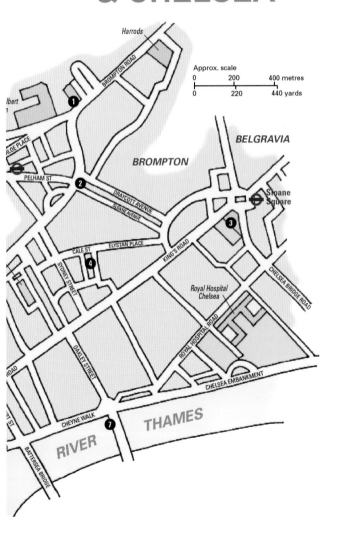

Harrods

Approx. scale

| 0 | 200 | 400 metres |
| 0 | 220 | 440 yards |

Albert

BELGRAVIA

BROMPTON

PELHAM ST

DRAYCOTT AVENUE

SLOANE AVENUE

Sloane Square

CALE ST

ELYSTAN PLACE

STONEY STREET

KING'S ROAD

CHELSEA BRIDGE ROAD

Royal Hospital Chelsea

OAKLEY STREET

ROYAL HOSPITAL ROAD

CHELSEA EMBANKMENT

CHEYNE WALK

THAMES

RIVER

BATTERSEA BRIDGE

Address: **Brompton Road, SW7 2RP (020-7808 0900, bromptonoratory.co.uk)**

Opening hours: **Daily 6am-8pm. Tours can be arranged. See website for service times.**

Cost: **free**

Transport: **South Kensington tube**

BROMPTON ORATORY

The Church of the Immaculate Heart of Mary – popularly known as the Brompton Oratory – is a stunning Roman Catholic church on Brompton Road next to the Victoria and Albert Museum. It's the church of a community of priests (lay brothers) called 'The Congregation of the Oratory of St Philip Neri' or Oratorians. Neri (1515-1595) founded his congregation in Rome, which spread worldwide and now numbers around 70 'houses' (including Birmingham and Oxford) with some 500 priests.

The Oratory was designed by Herbert Gribble (1847-1894, who won a design competition at the age of just 28), and the unabashed Italian style and ebullient design are entirely intentional. Construction commenced in 1878 and it was consecrated in 1884, although the remarkable dome, designed by George Sherrin (1843-1909) in neo-Baroque style, wasn't completed until 1896. The result is a church that's unique in Britain, particularly in its use of decorative colour and structure.

The Oratory is the second-largest Catholic church in London, with a nave wider than St Paul's Cathedral (exceeded in Britain only by Westminster Abbey and York Minster). Until the opening of Westminster Cathedral in 1903, the London Oratory was the venue for all great Catholic occasions in London.

Much of the interior decoration is of 20th-century provenance and isn't as Gribble intended; the lavishly-gilded nave and dome mosaics (1927-32) are the work of C.T.G. Formilli. Although

> As impressive as the exterior is, it's the extraordinary interior – where Italian influence is at its greatest – that takes the breath away.

the dome is striking, it's the pulpit that really catches the eye; this baroque wonder is alive with flowing lines and extravagant decoration, rarely seen in British churches. There's a beautiful altarpiece by Rex Whistler (1905-1944) in St Wilfrid's Chapel.

The Oratory is primarily 19th-century, but it contains a number of much older elements, including the figures of the 12 apostles in the nave, which were carved for Siena cathedral in 1680; the altar and reredos in the Lady Chapel are also from the late 17th century. Taken as a whole, the Brompton Oratory is an extraordinary architectural monument, made even more remarkable by the fact that such extravagant Italian style is so rare in Britain.

The church is also noted for the excellence of its liturgical and musical traditions. Its organ (1954, J.W. Walker & Sons) is one of the most important built in London in the post-World War Two period, and the church is graced by three renowned choirs.

Address: 81 Fulham Road, SW3 6RD (020-7581 5817, bibendum.co.uk)

Opening hours: Oyster Bar open seven days a week for coffee, breakfast, lunch or dinner; Claude Bosi restaurant, lunch Thu-Sun, dinner Wed-Sun, closed Mon-Tue. See website for times.

Cost: free, apart from the cost of a drink or meal (expensive!)

Transport: South Kensington tube

MICHELIN HOUSE

Michelin House was built as the permanent UK headquarters and tyre depot of the Michelin Tyre Company Ltd. and opened in 1911. Designed by one of Michelin's employees, François Espinasse (1880-1925), the original building had three large stained-glass windows based on Michelin adverts of the time, featuring the Michelin Man. At street level, there are a number of decorative ceramic tiles (which wrap around the front of the building) of famous racing cars which used Michelin tyres. One of the Michelin company's other passions is maps, which are represented by etchings of the streets of Paris on some of the first floor windows.

Walking into the reception area of the building, you're greeted by a mosaic on the floor showing Bibendum (the corpulent 'Michelin Man') holding aloft a glass of nuts, bolts and other hazards proclaiming *Nunc Est Bibendum* – Latin for 'now is the time to drink'. The reception area features more decorative tiles around its walls, while two glass cupolas, which look like piles of tyres, frame either side of the front of the building.

Michelin House is known for its decorative design, but it's also an early example of reinforced concrete construction. It was designed and built at the end of the Art Nouveau period, which is apparent in the decorative metalwork above the tyre-fitting bays, the tangling plants around the tyre motifs and the mosaic in the entrance hall. However, it's very like an Art Deco building, the popular style of the 1930s, with its strong advertising images, albeit one 20 years ahead of its time.

> Michelin House's exuberant, stylistic, individualism has variously been described as Art Nouveau, proto-Art Deco, Secessionist Functionalism and geometrical Classicism.

Michelin vacated the building in 1985, when it was purchased by the late publisher Paul Hamlyn (1926-2001) and restaurateur and retailer Sir Terence Conran (b 1931). The pair shared a love of the building for many years and embarked on a major redevelopment, which included restoring many of its original features (unfortunately the original stained-glass windows were removed during World War Two and then lost!). The new development contains offices, a shop, and the Bibendum Restaurant & Oyster Bar – which opened in August 1987. As befits such a beautiful building, Bibendum is now run by French chef Claude Bosi, who (appropriately) has two Michelin stars.

Address: Duke of York's HQ, King's Road, SW3 4RY (020-7811 3070, saatchigallery.com)

Opening hours: daily 10am-6pm, but check as it's frequently closed for private events

Cost: free (except for special exhibitions)

Transport: Sloane Square tube

SAATCHI GALLERY

The Saatchi Gallery was founded by advertising guru (and ex-husband of TV cook Nigella Lawson) Charles Saatchi in 1985 to exhibit his private collection of contemporary art. It has occupied various premises, first in north London, then the South Bank by the Thames, before moving to its current home at the Duke of York's HQ in Chelsea. Saatchi's collection (and hence the gallery's shows) has had distinct phases, starting with US artists and minimalism, moving to the Damien Hirst-led 'Young British Artists', followed by shows purely of painting, and then various avant-garde and multi-media shows displaying the work of emerging international artists.

The gallery has been a major influence on art in Britain since its opening and has had a history of media controversy, which it has courted, with extremes of critical reaction. Many artists on display are unknown, not only to the general public but also in the commercial art world, and showing at the gallery has provided a springboard for many artists' careers.

The collection's home, the Duke of York's Headquarters, was completed in 1801 to the designs of John Sanders (1768-1826), and is Grade II* listed, due to its outstanding historic and special architectural merit. It was originally called the Royal Military Asylum, a school for the children of soldiers' widows, but in 1892 was renamed the Duke of York's Royal Military School. In 1909, the school moved to new premises and it was renamed the Duke of York's Barracks. The site was purchased by Cadogan Estates in 2000 and redeveloped to include a public square, upmarket housing and retail outlets, part of which is now home to the Saatchi Gallery.

In 2010, it was announced that Charles Saatchi is to give the gallery – which will become the Museum of Contemporary Art for London – and some 200 works to the nation on his retirement.

On 9th October 2008, the Saatchi Gallery opened in its new premises, hailed as one of 'the most beautiful art space in London'. It's an ideal environment to view contemporary art, with large, well-proportioned rooms and high ceilings, arranged over three floors, providing some 70,000ft² (6,500m²) of space, with 15 equally-proportioned exhibition spaces. The gallery is one of largest (mostly free) contemporary art museums in the world, attracting over 1½ million visitors annually.

The Gallery Mess restaurant, bar and café has attracted enthusiastic reviews for its beautiful setting, atmosphere and food. There are also educational facilities and a bookshop.

Address: Sydney Street, SW3 6NH (020-7352 1201, chelseaparish.org)
Opening hours: Mon-Fri 9am-4pm. See website for service times.
Cost: free
Transport: South Kensington or Sloane Square tube

ST LUKE'S CHURCH & GARDEN

St Luke's (Grade I listed, with Grade II listed gardens) was built in 1824 to cater to a growing congregation, which had out-grown its parish church (now Chelsea Old Church – see **Cheyne Walk** on page 99). Designed by John Savage (1799-1852), it's built of Bath stone with flying buttresses and Gothic perpendicular towers along the nave and to the east end. It was one of the first Neo-Gothic churches built in London, with a 60ft (18.3m) high nave, the tallest of any parish church in London. Savage was one of the foremost authorities on medieval architecture, and the church has a grandeur of conception and great attention to detail. The interior was laid out in the traditional 18th-century manner of a preaching house, with an enormous pulpit, pews everywhere and a diminutive altar, although it was redesigned in the late 19th century to substantially what you see today.

The stunning east window, designed by Hugh Easton in honour of the Trinity and the Church, was installed in 1959 to replace one destroyed during World War Two, while the painting behind the altar depicts the deposition of Christ from the cross and is by James Northcote (1746-1831), a noted portrait painter. The two large sculptures (Stephen Cox, 1997) on either side of the altar represent Adam and Eve at the fall of man in the Garden of Eden, bowing their heads in shame for their disobedience to God.

St Luke's has a fine organ built by John Compton in 1932 (incorporating some parts from the original 1824 organ), which served as the prototype for organs at Broadcasting House and Downside Abbey; the church is also noted for the excellence of its choirs (both St Luke's and Christ Church). The church has a ring of ten bells in the tower, which were cast at Whitechapel when the church was built.

> The church has associations with many famous people, not least Charles Dickens, who married Catherine Hogarth here in 1836; the wedding took place two days after the publication of the first part of *The Pickwick Papers*.

The large burial ground which surrounded the church was converted into a public garden in 1881, with the gravestones forming a boundary wall. Today the delightful **garden is** known for its **beautiful flower beds and lovely trees (visit in** spring when they're in blossom), and is a welcome retreat from the surrounding streets. The garden also has a children's playground and a games area.

AT A GLANCE

Address: Fulham Road, SW10 9UG (020-7352 1201, royalparks.org.uk/parks/brompton-cemetery and brompton-cemetery.org.uk)

Opening hours: Daily 7am-dusk (8pm in summer, 4pm in winter). Guided tours (two hours) are held on certain Sundays (see brompton-cemetery.org.uk), for which there's a 'donation' of £8 per person towards the work of the Friends of Brompton Cemetery.

Cost: free

Transport: West Brompton tube

BROMPTON CEMETERY

Brompton Cemetery is one of Britain's oldest and most distinguished garden cemeteries, containing some 35,000 monuments which mark the sites of over 200,000 burials. It's Grade I listed, as are five individual monuments. People from all walks of life are buried here, including no fewer than 13 Victoria Cross holders. Among its most famous 'residents' are Beatrix Potter – she lived in 'The Boltons' nearby – who took the names of many of her animal characters from tombstones in the cemetery. It's also the last resting place of George Borrow, Henry Cole, Samuel Cunard, George Henty, Bernard Levin, Emmeline Pankhurst, Dr John Snow, Samuel Leigh Sotheby, Richard Tauber and John Wisden.

In the mid-19th century London's existing burial grounds, mostly churchyards, had long been unable to cope with the number of burials, and were a health hazard and an undignified way to treat the dead. Parliament established the creation of seven large, private cemeteries around London – which came to be called the 'Magnificent Seven' – of which Brompton is an outstanding example. The 39-acre (15.8ha) site lies between Old Brompton Road (North Gate) and Fulham Road (South Gate), which at the time was a distant suburb but is now a populous and diverse community close to central London.

The West London and Westminster Cemetery, as it was originally called, was established in 1836 and opened in 1840. Designed by Benjamin

> The Gothic splendour of Brompton Cemetery has proved irresistible to film-makers and it has been the backdrop for many period dramas, romantic comedies and thrillers.

Baud (1807-1875), it was regarded as one of the finest Victorian metropolitan cemeteries in the country, with a formal layout with a tree-lined central avenue leading to a domed chapel. The cemetery has the feel of a large open-air cathedral, with a central 'nave' and two long colonnades embracing the Great Circle, reputedly inspired by the piazza of St Peter's, Rome. Below the colonnades are catacombs, which were conceived as a cheaper alternative burial to having a plot, although they weren't a success and fewer than 500 were sold.

Today the cemetery is managed by the Royal Parks and is the only Crown Cemetery still used for burials, although most people use it as a public park rather than a place for mourning the dead. As well as its many attractions, the cemetery provides an oasis in all seasons and is a rare haven of peace, beauty and tranquillity in a part of London with few other green spaces.

AT A GLANCE

Address: **Chelsea, SW3 & SW10 (en.wikipedia.org/wiki/cheyne_walk)**
Opening hours: **unrestricted access**
Cost: **free**
Transport: **Sloane Square or South Kensington tube**

CHEYNE WALK

Cheyne Walk is an elegant, historic Thameside street in Chelsea, which takes its name from William Lord Cheyne (1657-1728), who owned the manor of Chelsea until 1712. Most of today's houses were built in the early 17th and 18th centuries when they fronted the Thames, long before the Embankment (which now fronts it) was constructed in the 19th century.

One of the most interesting and bizarre buildings on Cheyne Walk is Crosby Hall, which started life in Bishopsgate (City of London), where it was the Great Hall of 15th-century Crosby Place, owned by Sir John Crosby (d 1476), a wealthy wool merchant. The Hall was moved stone-by-stone from Bishopsgate to Chelsea in 1910 to rescue it from demolition, where it was incorporated into the buildings of the British Federation of University Women (used as a dining hall). It's now a private residence and stands next to the site of Sir Thomas More's former home.

One of Cheyne Walk's most prominent buildings is Carlyle Mansions, an apartment block built in 1886 and named after Thomas Carlyle, a resident of Chelsea for much of his life. It's appropriately dubbed 'Writers' Block' and has

> Sir Thomas More (1478-1535) was probably the first prominent resident of this riverside community, moving to a grand new home in 1520, later known as Beaufort House. Henry VIII soon followed and built a manor house as a wedding present for Catherine Parr in the 1540s, which later became the home of Elizabeth I, Lady Jane Grey and Anne of Cleves.

been home to Henry James, Erskin Childers, T. S. Eliot, Somerset Maugham and Ian Fleming, among other noted authors.

The list of residents and former residents of Cheyne Walk reads like *Who's Who* and includes (in addition to those mentioned above): JMW Turner, James Abbott Whistler, William Holman Hunt, Dante Gabriel Rossetti, Bryan Adams, David Lloyd George, Gerald Scarfe, Sylvia Pankhurst, George Best, Mick Jagger, Marianne Faithful, Bram Stoker, Sir Paul Getty II, George Eliot, Keith Richards, David Bowie, Ralph Vaughan Williams, Sir Hans Sloane, Elizabeth Gaskell, Diana Mitford, Sir Marc Brunel & his son Isambard Kingdom Brunel, Hilaire Belloc, George Weidenfeld and Laurence Olivier (phew!).

Chelsea Old Church is another of Cheyne Walk's many attractions, situated at number 64. Dating from 1157 and formerly the parish church of Chelsea, it was almost completely destroyed in World War Two (reopened in 1954). Fortunately, the 1528 More Chapel, built for Sir Thomas More and his family, survived virtually intact.

AT A GLANCE

Address: **Chelsea, SW3 (en.wikipedia.org/wiki/albert_bridge, london)**
Opening hours: **unrestricted access**
Cost: **free**
Transport: **Sloane Square tube**

ALBERT BRIDGE

Albert Bridge is a Grade II* listed road bridge over the Thames in west London, connecting Chelsea on the north bank to Battersea on the south. Designed as a modified, cable-stayed bridge by Rowland Mason Ordish (1824-1886), when it opened in 1873 it was 41ft (12m) wide and 710ft (220m) long, with a 384ft 9in (117.27m) central span. However, Ordish's bridge proved to be structurally unsound and in 1884-1887 Sir Joseph Bazalgette (1819-1891) incorporated some design elements of a suspension bridge. Further strengthening work was carried out in 1973 by adding two concrete piers, which transformed the central span into a simple beam bridge; hence the bridge you see today is an unusual hybrid of three different styles.

Viewed from the river it resembles something from a 'Fantasia' Walt Disney film and has been described as a wedding cake and a surrealist fantasy, while the towers resemble minarets crossed with a spray of stays. In 1992, the bridge was rewired and painted in an unusual colour scheme designed to make it more conspicuous in poor visibility, and hence avoid collisions with shipping. At night it's illuminated by 4,000 LEDs, making it one of London's most striking landmarks.

Built as a toll bridge, it was commercially unsuccessful, and six years after opening it was taken into public ownership and the tolls scrapped. However, the tollbooths remain in place and today are the only surviving examples in London.

Albert Bridge is a fragile cast iron structure with timber decking, built like so many other London bridges for horses and carriages. Incorporating a roadway just 27ft (8.2m) wide and with its structural weaknesses, the bridge was ill-equipped to cope with the advent of

> The bridge was nicknamed 'The Trembling Lady' due to its tendency to vibrate when large numbers of people walked over it – signs at the entrances warn 'all troops must break step when marching over this bridge'!

motor vehicles in the 20th century. Despite the many calls for its demolition or pedestrianisation, it has remained open to vehicles throughout its existence, and is one of only two Thames road bridges in central London never to have been replaced.

However, the strengthening work and re-designs were unable to prevent further deterioration, which has led to increasingly strict traffic control measures in order to prolong its life, including a weight limit of 2½ tons. The bridge was temporarily closed to traffic on 15th February 2010 – for strengthening and refurbishment – and reopened in December 2011.

Address: 224-238 Kensington High Street, W8 6AG (020-3862 5900, designmuseum.org)

Opening hours: daily 10am-6pm, until 8pm first Friday of the month

Cost: free access to permanent exhibition; fee for temporary exhibitions

Transport: High Street Kensington tube

DESIGN MUSEUM

Founded in 1989 by Sir Terence Conran (b1931), the Design Museum was originally located on the south bank of the River Thames in the Shad Thames area in southeast London, from where it relocated to Kensington in 2016. The museum encompasses product, industrial, graphic, fashion and architectural design, and champions design and the impact it has on the world, while introducing you to the people behind it.

The museum is housed in the former (Grade II* listed) Commonwealth Institute building, which was designed by John Pawson (interior) and Rem Koolhaas of the Dutch practice OMA, who made the building fit for a 21st-century museum – with a striking copper-covered, hyperbolic paraboloid roof – while at the same time retaining its spatial qualities. The museum's £83 million new premises are three times larger than the previous building, containing the Swarovski Foundation Centre for Learning, the 202-seat Bakala Auditorium and a dedicated gallery to display its permanent collection.

The top floor houses a permanent display, 'Designer Maker User', with key objects from the museum's collection. It features some 1,000 items of 20th and 21st-century design viewed through the angles of the designer, manufacturer and user, including a crowdsourced wall. The exhibition covers a broad range of design disciplines, from architecture and engineering, to the digital world, fashion and graphics.

> The wall display at the entrance to the 'Designer Maker User' exhibition features over 200 nominated objects from 25 countries, which demonstrate the intimate relationships we have with everyday objects that shape our lives. They include a bible, Coca-Cola can, £5 banknote, rubber gloves and a plastic garden chair.

A restaurant, members' lounge, residency studio, and an events and gallery space are also located on the top floor. On the first floor, a design and architecture reference library is a resource for students, educators, researchers and designers, while the Swarovski Foundation Centre for Learning encompasses a suite of learning facilities including a Design Studio, Creative Workshop, two seminar rooms and a Common Room. On the ground floor, the museum's largest gallery showcases a programme of temporary exhibitions.

A double-height space spanning the two lower levels, Gallery Two hosts a programme of temporary exhibitions dedicated to architecture, fashion, furniture, product and graphic design. The Bakala Auditorium provides a purpose-designed space for a programme of talks, seminars, debates, and public and private events throughout the year.

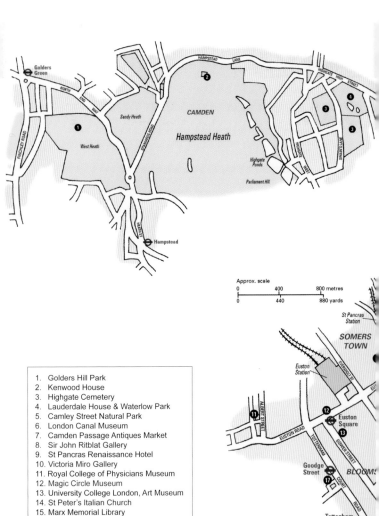

1. Golders Hill Park
2. Kenwood House
3. Highgate Cemetery
4. Lauderdale House & Waterlow Park
5. Camley Street Natural Park
6. London Canal Museum
7. Camden Passage Antiques Market
8. Sir John Ritblat Gallery
9. St Pancras Renaissance Hotel
10. Victoria Miro Gallery
11. Royal College of Physicians Museum
12. Magic Circle Museum
13. University College London, Art Museum
14. St Peter's Italian Church
15. Marx Memorial Library
16. Museum of the Order of St John
17. Pollock's Toy Museum
18. St Etheldreda's
19. Phoenix Garden
20. Freemasons' Hall & Museum
21. Postal Museum & Mail Rail

CHAPTER 4

CAMDEN & ISLINGTON

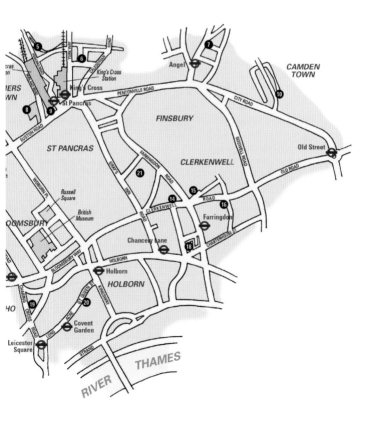

AT A GLANCE

Address: West Heath Avenue, NW11 7QP (020-7332 3511, cityoflondon. gov.uk > Hampstead Heath > Golders Hill Park)

Opening hours: Park & zoo, daily 7.30am-dusk; Butterfly house, March-October, daily 1-3pm (see website for exact dates)

Cost: free

Transport: Golders Green tube

GOLDERS HILL PARK

G olders Hill Park is a formal park in Golders Green, part of
the parkland and commons in and near Hampstead Heath,
as well as part of Hampstead Heath Local Nature Reserve.
It was opened to the public in 1898 and has been managed as a
separate part of Hampstead Heath by the City of London since
1989 (unlike the rest of the heath, Golders Hill Park is closed
at night). It adjoins the West Heath and is on a site formerly
occupied by a large 18th-century house (created in the 1760s by
Charles Dingley) which was destroyed during World War Two.

The main characteristic of the park is a large expanse of grass
(great for games), dotted with specimen trees, a beautiful formal
English flower garden and a water garden with a number of
ponds. The ponds are stocked with marsh and water plants, and
a large number of water birds, including black and white swans.
Formal paths wind their way around the park, criss-crossing and
meandering beneath beautiful trees, past ponds, through secret
vales and a free children's zoo.

The zoo plays an important role in the interpretation and
education of the habitats and wildlife of Hampstead Heath, and
has a growing collection of rare and exotic birds and mammals
from all corners of the globe, including alpaca, kookaburras,
Patagonian maras, red-legged seriemas, white-naped cranes,
ring-tailed lemurs and coatis, plus fallow deer in a large enclosure.
There's also a Butterfly House, which allows a close-up of
many British and tropical species, where you can study the life
cycle of these fascinating
insects, their habitats, food
chains, adaptation and
sustainability.

| During the summer, children's activities are organised and throughout June and July there's live music on the bandstand (brass bands, jazz, etc.) on Sunday afternoons. |

The park has an excellent
café (try the delicious
home-made ice-cream), a
bandstand, children's play
area, and a variety of sports and leisure facilities, including (hard)
tennis courts, a croquet lawn, golf practice nets and a putting
green.

Golders Hill Park is a great place to spend a relaxing day
with the kids and is everything an urban park should be. Note,
however, that unlike most of Hampstead Heath, you must keep
your dog on a leash due to the animals.

If you have some spare time, why not visit splendid Hill Garden
& Pergola, a hidden treasure just five minutes stroll southeast of
the park (follow the signs from the park).

Address: Hampstead Lane, Hampstead, NW3 7JR (020-8348 1286, english-heritage.org.uk/visit/places/kenwood)

Opening hours: house 10am-4/6pm (see website for exact times), grounds 8am-dusk

Cost: free, tours £17.20/£13.40

Transport: Archway or Golders Green tube, then 210 bus

KENWOOD HOUSE

Tucked away in beautiful landscaped parkland on Hampstead Heath, Kenwood House (Grade II* listed) is one of the most magnificent estates in London, now managed by English Heritage. The elegant villa was built in the 17th century (c1616) and was owned for over 200 years by the family of William Murray, 1st Earl of Mansfield (1705-1793). It was remodelled by Robert Adam (1728-1792) between 1764 and 1773, who transformed the original brick house into a majestic neoclassical villa. Adam's richly decorated library, with its beautiful friezes and grand colonnades, is a masterpiece and considered one of the most important period rooms in the country. In 1793-6, George Saunders (1762-1839) added two wings on the north side and the offices, kitchen buildings and a brewery (now the restaurant).

Brewing magnate Edward Cecil Guinness, first Earl of Iveagh (1847-1927), bought Kenwood House and the remaining 74-acre estate in 1925, and on his death bequeathed the house, land and part of his collection of paintings to the nation. The Iveagh Bequest (as it's known) includes important paintings by great masters, including Rembrandt, Vermeer, Turner, Reynolds and Gainsborough, along with Constable's oil sketch 'Hampstead Heath'. The paintings beautifully complement Kenwood's sumptuous interiors and rich decoration, and it's also home to the Suffolk collection of rare Elizabethan portraits.

The parkland surrounding Kenwood was influenced by the renowned English landscape gardener Humphrey Repton (1752-1818), and was designed to be seen from a planned circuit walk that provided a series of evocative views, contrasts and 'surprises'. Although bordered on three sides by Hampstead

The gardens near the house contain a number of sculptures, including Barbara Hepworth's 'Monolith (Empyrean)' of 1959 at the west end of the lawn and Henry Moore's bronze 'Two Piece Reclining Figure' of 1963-4 overlooking the lakes from the lawn.

Heath, the estate was maintained as a designed landscape until the '50s with a different character from the Heath. Highlights include the walled garden with its kidney shaped butterfly bed and ivy arch, leading from the flower garden to a raised terrace with stunning views over the lakes. The inner and outer circuit routes take you around lawns, over bridges and through woods, following the original paths created by Repton.

Set high on a hill, the panoramic views of London from Kenwood are stunning. What better way to spend a day than with lunch in the Brew House café followed by a walk across the hills of Hampstead Heath, taking in the sweeping views of the metropolis on the way.

Address: Swains Lane, N6 6PJ (020-8340 1834, highgate-cemetery.org)

Opening hours: East Cemetery: daily 10am-5pm (Mar-Oct), 10am-4pm (Nov-Feb). West Cemetery: entry by guided tour only (see website). Booking essential Mon-Fri, weekends no bookings but limited places.

Cost: East Cemetery (unaccompanied) £4; West Cemetery tours, adults £12, child 8-17 £6, under 8s not permitted

Transport: Highgate or Archway tube

Tomb of Karl Heinrich Marx

HIGHGATE CEMETERY

Highgate Cemetery (Grade I listed) opened in 1839, soon after Queen Victoria's accession to the throne, and was one of London's Magnificent Seven Cemeteries. It was designed by Stephen Geary (1797-1854) and landscaped by David Ramsey with exotic formal planting, although it was the stunning architecture that made Highgate the capital's principal and most fashionable cemetery, further enhanced by its unparalleled elevation overlooking London.

Two chapels were built in the Tudor style, topped with wooden turrets and a central bell tower. In the heart of the grounds was created the splendid Egyptian Avenue, with vaults on either side of a passageway entered via a great arch, inspired by the recent discovery of the Valley of the Kings in Egypt. This leads to the eerie Circle of Lebanon (surrounding a huge cedar of Lebanon tree, some 300 years old), a ring of vaults and catacombs completed in 1842 in the Gothic style. The cemetery is divided into two parts, the East (opened in 1856) and West (the original) cemeteries, encompassing a total area of 37 acres (15ha).

By the turn of the century the desire for elaborate funerals was waning, and by the 1930s Highgate was in decline. After years of neglect, the cemetery was saved in 1975 by the Friends of Highgate Cemetery. Over the last four decades there has been extensive restoration

In the 19th century cemeteries were more than simply a place for burials; they were a popular tourist attraction where thousands came to admire the memorials and tombs, and somewhere to be enjoyed for their beauty and peacefulness.

and conservation, including several lavish (listed) monuments. Among the prominent figures buried here are the family of Charles Dickens, Michael Faraday, Karl Marx, Christina Rossetti, Douglas Adams, George Eliot, Malcolm McLaren, Sir Ralph Richardson, Max Wall, John Galsworthy and six Lord Mayors of London.

While the East Cemetery is a pleasant place for a stroll, it's the much murkier and foreboding West Cemetery – accessible only by guided tour to protect the monuments – that is the dark soul of Highgate, containing a wealth of Gothic monuments overgrown with ivy and moss in a scene reminiscent of a horror movie. Its confusion of plants, trees and memorials has become a wildlife sanctuary, where foxes, hedgehogs, butterflies, insects and birds thrive in the heart of London.

Apart from being one of London's historical treasures, Highgate Cemetery is a haven of beauty and tranquillity, a world away from life beyond its walls.

AT A GLANCE

Address: Lauderdale House, Highgate Hill, N6 5HG (house: 020-8348 8716, lauderdalehouse.co.uk, waterlowpark.org.uk)

Opening hours: park, dawn to dusk; house, Mon-Fri 11am-4pm, closed Sat-Sun; café, Mon-Fri 8.30am-5pm, Sat-Sun 9.30am-5.30pm

Cost: free

Transport: Archway or Highgate tube

LAUDERDALE HOUSE & WATERLOW PARK

Lauderdale House was built in 1582 for Sir Richard Martin (d 1617), the Master of the Mint and three-time Lord Mayor of London, and has a rich and interesting history. Over the next 60 years it had a number of occupants, until Mary, Dowager Countess of Home, bequeathed it to her daughter Anne, wife of the Scottish Royalist John Maitland, the notorious Earl of Lauderdale (1616-1682), thus beginning the connection with the name. Charles II's mistress Nell Gwynn lived here for a brief period with their infant son, the Duke of St Albans. Over the next century or so the House changed hands many times and was described by John Wesley, who preached here in 1782, as 'one of the most elegant boarding houses in England.'

Lauderdale's last private owner was Sir Sidney Waterlow (1822-1906), after whom the park is named, who leased the house for a period to St Bartholomew's Hospital as a convalescent home. By 1883 the house lay empty and in 1889 Sir Sidney gave the house and grounds to the London County Council 'for the enjoyment of Londoners' and as 'a garden for the gardenless'. The 29 acres (11.7ha) of land became a public park and the house was restored in 1893 and served for 70 years as a park tearoom and park-keepers' flats. During the course of further renovation in 1963, a fire destroyed the roof and much of the interior. After 15 years lying derelict the local community established the Lauderdale House Society, which now runs the house as an arts and education centre (see website) – with an excellent café.

> Nestled on a hillside to the south of Highgate Village, Waterlow Park has some of the best cityscape views in London, but retains a wonderful sense of peace and serenity.

Separately managed by Camden Council, Waterlow Park – returned to its former glory after extensive restoration in 2005 – is one of a select group of parks awarded Green Flag status and one of London's best-kept secrets.

Within its expansive acreage you'll find a potpourri of formal terraced gardens (one of Britain's earliest examples); three historic ponds fed by natural springs; tree-lined walkways and mature shrub beds; herbaceous borders and ornamental bedding; and verdant expanses of lawn on which to play, relax or have a picnic. The park also boasts six tennis courts, a natural children's play area and an ever-changing events programme.

Address: 12 Camley Street, NW1 0PW (020-3897 6150, wildlondon.org.uk/reserves/camley-street-natural-park)

Opening hours: 10am-5pm

Cost: free

Transport: King's Crosss St Pancras tube/rail

CAMLEY STREET NATURAL PARK

C amley Street Natural Park is a tranquil green area in the most urban of locations, situated immediately behind St Pancras International Station. This internationally-acclaimed reserve was awarded Green Flag status in 2009 and is a special place for both people and wildlife and well worth a visit.

Comprising 2 acres (0.8ha) of land on the banks of the Regent's Canal – alongside St Pancras Lock – Camley Street Natural Park is an urban wildlife sanctuary and education centre run by the London Wildlife Trust. The park opened in 1985 and is a legacy of the pioneering conservation projects established by the former Greater London Council's 'London Ecology Unit'. It's an example of the success and importance of urban ecology for environmental and educational purposes in the heart of London. The site was a coal depot from Victorian times until the '60s, when it became derelict, and was acquired in 1981 by the Greater London Council for a lorry/coach park; however, local people, along with the London Wildlife Trust, successfully campaigned against this proposal.

In 1988 its future was threatened again when the King's Cross railway lands were designated for redevelopment for the Channel Tunnel Rail Link (and Eurostar station), which resulted in some land being lost in the south, although an additional area was added in the southeast corner. The park's shape comprises a narrow strip of land bounded by the canal, Camley Street and Goods Way, with the entrance via an ornate gate on Camley Street.

A variety of habitats co-exists in the park's relatively small area, including wetlands, marshland, a wild flower meadow, woodland, reed beds around a pond and a garden area, all of which attract a wealth of insects (including many butterflies), amphibians, birds, mammals and a rich variety of plant life.

The park is popular with those seeking respite from the noise and bustle of the city, as well as a hub for London Wildlife Trust volunteers

Some of the reserve's stars include the rare earthstar fungi, bats and around 50 bird species, including reed warblers, kingfishers, geese, mallards and reed buntings.

(it has a full-time education programme for Camden schools). A visitors' centre caters for casual visitors and school parties, although tours must be booked.

A pedestrian bridge now spans the Regent's Canal, connecting Granary Square and King's Cross with Camley Street Natural Park and Somers Town.

AT A GLANCE

Address: 12/13 New Wharf Road, N1 9RT (020-7713 0836, canalmuseum. org.uk)

Opening hours: Tue-Sun 10am-4.30pm (7.30pm on the first Thu of each month), closed Mon (except bank holidays)

Cost: **adults £5, concessions £4, children £2.50, families £12.50**

Transport: **King's Cross tube**

LONDON CANAL MUSEUM

The London Canal Museum tells the absorbing story of the capital's canals from their early days as vital trade routes – long before motorised vehicles and motorways – through years of decline and abandonment, to their resurrection as today's corridors of leisure and urban greenery for boats, walkers and cyclists.

The museum opened in 1992 in a former Victorian ice warehouse, constructed around 1863 by Carlo Gatti (a famous ice-cream maker) to house ice imported from Norway by ship and canal barge. The museum features two floors of exhibits, including half a narrow boat, the *Coronis*, which allows you to experience the cramped conditions in which boatmen and their families lived (from the 1840s until the 1950s); there are also some fascinating recordings, displays and photographs of a way of life, now long gone.

Outside, in Battlebridge Basin, is moored the museum's own tug, *Bantam IV* (plus private narrowboats), while upstairs is a detailed history of how the canals developed and were engineered, fascinating archival film footage on a continuous loop and a mechanical model lock. Further exhibits explain the role of lock keepers, reservoirs and horses, the backbone of the early canal network. The museum also contains a copy of a drawing by Leonardo da Vinci, inventor of the mitre gate that's still used today in most of the world's locks. As an added bonus, there are two preserved ice wells under the building, one of which can be viewed from the public area.

> From the River Thames at Limehouse to Paddington, the nine-mile Regent's Canal is one of London's best-kept secrets, largely hidden behind high-rise buildings.

The museum tells the story of the building of Regent's (London) Canal – built to link the Grand Junction Canal's Paddington Arm (which opened in 1801) with the Thames at Limehouse – in texts, pictures and archive film from the 1920s to 1940s. You can get an excellent overview of the scope of London's waterways from the 'Big Map', which provides a detailed historical survey of the capital's canals and other navigations, including canals that were built and closed, those that were planned but never built, and those that survive today.

Visitors to the museum can take a short tunnel trip on a narrow boat through Islington Tunnel to Regent's Canal (on selected summer Sundays – see website), or go the whole hog and take an enchanting trip back in time from Camden to picturesque Little Venice in west London, meandering through the rich urban landscape of yesteryear.

Address: **Camden Passage, The Angel, N1 8EA (camdenpassageislington. co.uk)**

Opening hours: **main market Wed & Sat 9am-6pm, sporadic opening on Fri & Sun**

Cost: **free**

Transport: **Angel tube**

CAMDEN PASSAGE ANTIQUES MARKET

Camden Passage is a pedestrian passage built as an alley along the backs of houses on Upper Street (then Islington High Street) in the mid-18th century. Hidden down a cobblestoned Angel backstreet, visiting the Passage is like stepping back in time. On market days you'll find a multitude of stalls selling an eclectic mix of antiques and collectibles – vintage clothes, handbags, jewellery, silver, porcelain, glass and assorted bric-a-brac – intermingled with a range of elegant Georgian antiques shops, pubs, cafés and restaurants.

Whether you're a dealer, interior designer, collector or just a curious browser, you'll find Camden Passage intriguing. Most of the traders are specialists who know their stuff, so just chatting to them can be an education as well as a lot of fun, but you'll need to arrive early to pick over the stalls or haggle hard to get a bargain.

The Passage's current incarnation dates back to the early '60s, when local businessman John Payton had a vision that it would make a great antiques market. With the assistance of local shopkeepers, antiques centres were created from bomb sites and arcades of small shops built. Antiques dealers soon flocked to the area creating a unique antiques village, which at its peak boasted some 350 dealers.

Nowadays the market is much smaller, but what it lacks in quantity it more than makes up for in quality, with a unique collection of traders of all types and levels. Today's specialist dealers include Vincent Freeman (no. 1), music boxes, singing

> Enthusiasts can spend a delightful morning or afternoon browsing the shops and stalls, stopping for a coffee or beer in one of the local hostelries (such as the Camden Head) – or even better – lunch in one of the excellent cafés or restaurants.

birds and automata; Kevin Page's Oriental Art (nos. 2-4), one of London's leading dealers in Chinese and Japanese antiques; Mike Weedon (no. 7), Art Deco, Art Nouveau and European ceramics; and Piers Rankin (no. 14), silver and Sheffield plate. The camaraderie of the traders has ensured that the Passage has survived where other antiques areas have failed. Standards have remained high and the wide range of quality goods on offer has ensured its enduring success as a centre of excellence.

Camden Passage Antiques Market (not to be confused with the much larger Camden Markets in Camden Town) is open on Wednesdays and Saturdays, although the larger antique shops also open on other days or by appointment.

Address: **The British Library, 96 Euston Road, NW1 2DB (020-7412 7332, bl.uk/events/treasures-of-the-british-library)**

Opening hours: **Mon-Fri 9.30am-6pm (8pm Tue), Sat 9.30am-5pm, Sun and most public holidays 11am-5pm**

Cost: **free**

Transport: **King's Cross St Pancras tube/rail**

15th-century Macclesfield Alphabet book

SIR JOHN RITBLAT GALLERY

The Sir John Ritblat Gallery – sub-titled 'Treasures of the British Library' – is named after a major donor who also provided £1 million for the library's display cabinets, and is a permanent display of some of the world's rarest and most precious manuscripts and books. It contains over 200 beautiful and fascinating items, including sacred texts from the world's religions, documents that made and recorded history, landmarks of printing, masterpieces of illumination, major advances in science and map-making, and great works of literature and music.

Discover some of the world's most exciting and significant books and documents, from the *Lindisfarne Gospels* (698AD), with their wonderful illustrations, to the *Gutenberg Bible* (1455), the first book printed in Europe. From the genius of Leonardo da Vinci's sketchbooks to the earliest versions of some of the greatest works of English literature, including Shakespeare's *First Folio* (1623), Jane Austen's *History of England* (1791) and Lewis Carroll's *Alice in Wonderland* (1865). Also on display is the *Diamond Sutra*, the world's earliest dated printed book, made with carved wood blocks in 868AD, the only surviving copy of the epic poem *Beowulf*, thought to date from the 10th or 11th century, and the Earl of Essex's death warrant (1601) signed by Elizabeth I.

Among the most important documents on display is the *Magna Carta* – considered by many historians to be the greatest constitutional document of all time – which King John was compelled to sign by his feudal barons in 1215, accepting that no 'freeman' (in the sense of non-serf) could be punished except through the law of the land – a right which still exists today.

A room off the main gallery houses the 'Turning the Pages' system, where you can scan selected books on a computer terminal, such as the *Lindisfarne Gospels*, the *Sforza Hours* – one of the finest surviving Renaissance manuscripts – the *Diamond Sutra* and da Vinci's notebook, as if you were actually turning the books' pages.

The gallery also includes musical scores by the likes of Bach, Handel and Mozart, Beethoven's tuning fork, and scribbled lyrics of Lennon and McCartney, such as *A Hard Day's Night*, written on a sheet of stationery picturing a cartoon train. Also in the British Library is the National Sound Archive – where you can hear recordings of Florence Nightingale (1890) and James Joyce reading from *Ulysses* (1924) – and the Humanities Reading Room.

There's a café and an excellent restaurant within the library, the latter offering superb views of the King's Library.

AT A GLANCE

Address: Euston Road, NW1 2AR (020-7841 3540, stpancraslondon.com)

Opening hours: hotel 24 hours; public tours (one hour) are organised on weekends (bookings, 020-8241 6921) and private tours are also available upon request

Cost: tours £24, maximum of 15 people. Or you can have a drink or a coffee in the Booking Office Bar if you just want to have a look around.

Transport: King's Cross St Pancras tube/rail

ST PANCRAS RENAISSANCE HOTEL

The St Pancras Renaissance Hotel opened in May 2011, occupying the lower floors of the former Midland Grand Hotel (1873-1935) – dubbed London's most romantic building – including the main public rooms and 38 original bedrooms and suites. A completely new bedroom wing was also added, while the upper levels of the original building were re-developed as apartments by the Manhattan Loft Corporation.

The Midland Grand Hotel – designed by the prolific architect Sir George Gilbert Scott (1811-1878) and opened in 1873 – was all about romance, grandeur and style. It was luxurious and expensive with costly fixtures including a grand staircase, gold leaf walls and a fireplace in each room. The building had many innovative features such as hydraulic lifts, concrete floors, revolving doors and a fireproof floor construction, although, as was the convention at the time, none of the guest rooms had private bathrooms.

The hotel was taken over by the London Midland and Scottish Railway in 1922, before closing in 1935, by which time it was outdated and too expensive to maintain. It was renamed St Pancras Chambers and used as offices by British Rail until the '80s, when it failed the fire safety regulations and was closed. For years, the building lay mothballed and abandoned.

In the '90s the fairy-tale red façade was restored at a cost of around £10 million and planning permission granted (in 2005) for the building to be redeveloped as a new hotel and residential apartments. After years of dedicated restoration – costing an eye-watering £150 million – the building was resurrected in 2011 as the 5-star St Pancras Renaissance Hotel.

Scott's wide stone cantilevered staircase – which has featured in many films – has been sandblasted and its

> Today the glorious Gothic Revival metalwork, gold leaf ceilings, hand-stencilled wall designs and the grand staircase are as dazzling as the day the Midland Grand Hotel first opened.

intricate balustrade polished. On each floor, rooms open up to reveal elaborate and unique detailing. The covered, arched former taxi rank has been artfully re-designed to create a reception area, and the adjoining old ticket hall, with its dark-panelled walls and soaring church-like windows, is now a bar. The hotel's fine-dining restaurant (occupying the original grand restaurant space) is appropriately named The Gilbert Scott, run by celebrated chef Marcus Wareing.

Sir John Betjeman called this Gothic treasure 'too beautiful and too romantic to survive in a world of tower blocks and concrete'. Its survival against the odds is a triumph that will take your breath away.

Address: Address: 16 Wharf Road, N1 7RW (020-7336 8109, victoria-miro. com)

Opening hours: Tue-Sat 10am-6pm, closed Sun-Mon

Cost: free

Transport: Angel or Old Street tube

VICTORIA MIRO GALLERY

Victoria Miro is one of the *grandes dames* of the Britart scene. She first opened a contemporary art gallery in Cork Street, Mayfair in 1985, which earned widespread acclaim for showcasing the work of established and emerging artists from Europe, Asia and the US, and for nurturing the careers of young British artists. In 2000, the gallery relocated to its present home, a converted, 8,000ft² (743m²) furniture factory, with exhibition spaces on two floors.

The gallery occupies a small group of buildings which sit in the shabby no-man's land between two of London's most trendy areas, Islington and Hoxton. This ensemble embraces Victoria Miro's old and new gallery, plus the Parasol Unit Foundation for Contemporary Art. It's an astonishing gallery space; brilliantly lit, which seems to evoke the focused, grounded and slightly eccentric modernism of Portugal rather than the fussy minimalism of England or the trying-too-hard, boho-chic of New York.

In 2006, the gallery expanded further when it opened Victoria Miro 14 (designed by Michael Drain), a 9,000ft² (836m²) public exhibition and viewing space for special exhibitions and projects. It sits atop a refurbished Victorian building, its sculptural, minimalist form creating a dramatic approach to the building from the street. Illuminating the south façade through its 6-metre high windows is Ian Hamilton Finlay's elegiac, neon installation, *The Seas Leaves the Strawberries Waves* (1990). Inside, a triple-height staircase leads to the main space which affords spectacular views of the city from its floor-to-ceiling windows.

One of the largest commercial art spaces in London, the Victoria Miro Gallery represents established names such as film and installation artist Doug Aitken

> The gallery is almost unique in London for having its own garden, a beautiful landscaped area overlooking a restored stretch of the Regent's Canal, which has been used to great effect for installations by artists such as Yayoi Kusama (Japan).

and younger talent like Conrad Shawcross, and also works with the estates of artists such as Alice Neel. The gallery represents two winners of the Turner Prize: Chris Ofili, who won in 1998, and the 2003 winner, Grayson Perry, as well as four Turner Prize nominees: Ian Hamilton Finlay, Peter Doig, Isaac Julien and Phil Collins. After celebrating its 30th anniversary in 2015, the gallery ethos remains the same: to promote great and innovative artists and nurture the best talent from the new generation of artists around the world.

In 2013 Miro launched her second art gallery in London, Victoria Miro Mayfair, and in 2017 opened a third gallery in Venice.

Address: 11 St Andrews Place, NW1 4LE (020-3075 1200, rcplondon. ac.uk)

Opening hours: Mon-Fri 9am-5pm; guided tours (1 hour) for groups of 6-25 (bookings: history@rcplondon.ac.uk), free 30-minute tours 1.30pm and free garden tours (2pm) Mar-Oct on the first Wednesday of the month.

Cost: free, guided tours £8 per person

Transport: Great Portland Street, Regent's Park or Warren Street tube

ROYAL COLLEGE OF PHYSICIANS MUSEUM

The Royal College's collections cover its own history and that of the physician's profession, and helps to place the development of medicine and healthcare in its widest context. They include over 5,000 paintings, prints, drawings and sculptures (many displayed in the central marble hall and galleries): a silver collection, some still used during ceremonies, including the earliest known piece of English hallmarked silver, the Symons collection of medical instruments, the Hoffbrand collection of apothecary jars, commemorative medals and anatomical tables.

There's also a library containing over 30,000 items printed before 1900, although most of the College's original books were lost in the Great Fire. Each individual item has a story to tell and provides an insight into the continual movement for the advancement of healthcare. Visitors can also explore the College's medicinal garden containing over 1,300 plants.

The Royal College of Physicians of London was founded in 1518 as the College of Physicians (it acquired its 'Royal' prefix in 1674) by charter of Henry VIII. The main functions of the College were to grant licences to those qualified to practise – including apothecaries as well as physicians – and punish unqualified practitioners and those engaging in malpractice.

The first College was located at Amen Corner near St Paul's Cathedral and was destroyed in the Great Fire (1666). The College has had five homes in London since its foundation in 1518, moving to its fifth and present home in Regent's Park in 1964. Designed by Sir Denys Lasdun (1914-2001), who

> An interesting feature of the building is a 'Moving Wall', weighing five tons (5,080kg) and capable of being hydraulically lifted ten feet (3m) to unite or sub-divide a hall that's 62ft (18.9m) wide – the interior width of the building.

was awarded the Trustees Medal of the Royal Institute of British Architects in recognition of his work, it's one of very few Grade I listed post-war buildings.

Throughout its history the College has issued advice across the whole range of medical and health matters; it became the licensing body for medical books in the late 17th century and sought to set new standards in learning through its own system of examinations. The College has been continuously active in improving practice medicine ever since, primarily through training and qualifying new physicians, which continues to this day.

Address: **12 Stephenson Way, NW1 2HD (020-7367 2222, themagiccircle. co.uk)**

Opening hours: **check website for information about current events**

Cost: **varies – contact the museum for information**

Transport: **Euston rail and Euston Square tube**

MAGIC CIRCLE MUSEUM

Widely acclaimed as the finest magic headquarters in the world, The Magic Circle was founded in 1905 after a meeting of 23 amateur and professional magicians at Pinoli's restaurant, chaired by Servais Le Roy. Meetings were held in a room at St George's Hall in Langham Place, where magicians David Devant – the greatest magician of his era and the first president of the Circle – and Nevil Maskelyne regularly performed.

The Magic Circle later moved to its current home in Stephenson Way, a 7,000ft² (650m²) venue dubbed 'The Centre for the Magic Arts', designed and refurbished at a cost of £2.1 million. The building includes the Clubroom and the Devant Room, with showcases displaying unique apparatus of the past. At the top of the building, reached by a lift or the spectacular spiral staircase, is a fully-equipped theatre, where magic shows are presented.

The most priceless treasures, memorabilia and magical posters are displayed in a museum on the lower ground floor, which also houses lending and reference libraries containing the largest collection of magic books in Europe. The antiquarian library includes the first book on conjuring in the English language, Scott's *Discoverie of Witchcraft*.

Museum exhibits include magic tricks, props, posters, programmes, toys, photographs and artefacts related to magic and illusionists. You'll discover how the great illusionist

> Props include Harry Houdini's handcuffs and those used by HRH The Prince of Wales when he took his examination to become a member of The Magic Circle.

Chung Ling Soo was accidentally shot dead during a performance in 1918 at the Wood Green Empire, how the British army used a famous magician to make the Suez Canal 'invisible' to enemy bombers in 1941 and, if you look very closely, you might even see how a rabbit appears from a top hat. Items of interest include props used by TV magicians Tommy Cooper and David Nixon and a sound recording of Harry Houdini from an Edison cylinder.

The motto of the society is the Latin *indocilis privata loqui*, which roughly translates as 'not apt to disclose secrets'; members must give their word not to wilfully disclose magic secrets other than to bona fide students of magic – anyone breaking this or any other rule may be expelled!

The Magic Circle holds regular 'At Home with the Magic Circle' evenings – usually twice a month on Tuesdays – performed by some of the Circle's top magicians, plus many other public events throughout the year. There's also a Young Magicians Club (see youngmagiciansclub.co.uk).

Address: **South Cloisters, Wilkins Building, Gower Street, WC1E 6BT**
(020-7679 2540, ucl.ac.uk/culture/ucl-art-museum)

Opening hours: **Tue-Fri 1-5pm**

Cost: **free**

Transport: **Euston Square tube**

St Michael Overcoming Satan,
John Flaxman

UNIVERSITY COLLEGE LONDON, ART MUSEUM

This little-known museum has over 10,000 objects, many of international importance, including paintings, drawings, prints and sculptures dating from 1490 to the present day. Its home, University College London (UCL), is a public research university and the oldest and largest constituent college of the University of London.

The UCL Art Collections – renamed the UCL Art Museum in 2011 – date from 1847 when a collection of sculpture models and drawings of the Neo-classical artist John Flaxman (1755-1826) was obtained. Extensive gifts of prints and drawings were later donated, including the George Grote (1794-1871) bequest of 1872. Grote inherited his family's collection of bound albums containing early German, Flemish, Dutch and Italian drawings, as well as a large collection of prints. The collection includes important works by German 16th-century artists such as Hans Burgkmair, who worked for the court of the Holy Roman Emperor Maximilian in Augsburg, and Sigmund Holbein, uncle to the more famous Hans.

The Vaughan Bequest of 1900 included drawings by Turner and De Wint, Rembrandt etchings and early proofs and states (a type of proof) of Turner's Liber Studiorum and Constable's English Landscape Scenery. The Sherborn Bequest of 1937 added many rare and important prints to the collection, including an early edition of Dürer's Apocalypse woodcuts and early states and proofs from Van Dyck's Iconographia.

The collection also contains prize-winning student work from the nearby Slade School of Art, dating from 1890 to the present day, including works

> Founded in 1826, UCL was (surprisingly) the first university institution to be founded in London and the first in England established on an entirely secular basis, admitting students irrespective of their religion and women on equal terms with men and from 1878 could take degrees.

by many important 20th-century British artists such as Stanley Spencer, Augustus John, Edward Wadsworth and Paula Rego. The prize-winning student works were augmented by gifts of work by Slade staff and students, including Henry Tonks and David Bomberg, and the collection has been extended by recent purchase of works by Gwen John, Stanley Spencer and other Slade students.

Works on paper are housed in the Strang Print Room, while paintings and sculpture are displayed in public rooms around the college. The Strang Print Room is the administrative centre of the collection, functioning as an exhibition space, study and teaching room.

AT A GLANCE

Address: Chiesa Italiana di San Pietro, 136 Clerkenwell Road, EC1R 5DL (020-7837 1528, italianchurch.org.uk)

Opening hours: **Open all day on most days. If closed, visit the parish office (4 Back Hill) or telephone the office. See website for service times.**

Cost: **free**

Transport: **Farringdon or Chancery Lane tube**

ST PETER'S ITALIAN CHURCH

In the early 19th century the Saffron Hill area of London was a poor neighbourhood of densely populated slum-ridden alleys, whose inhabitants included some 2,000 Italian immigrants who worshipped at the Royal Sardinian Chapel, Lincoln's Inn Fields. In 1845, Vincent Pallotti (1795-1850), a Roman Catholic priest and founder of the **Societas Apostolatus Catholici** (Pallottine Fathers), had the idea of building a church for Italian immigrants. The Irish architect John Miller-Bryson was given the task and worked from plans drawn up by Francesco Gualandi of Bologna, which in turn were modelled on the Basilica of San Crisogono in Trastevere, Rome.

St Peter's opened amid great celebration on 16th April 1863, when it was the only church in Britain in the Roman Basilica style. It was originally the 'Church Of All Nations' and attracted congregations of many faiths and nationalities (a Polish chapel was established in the crypt), many drawn by the excellence of the music. The choir was outstanding and regular concerts were held, featuring distinguished soloists and orchestras. The Italian Church, as it became known, was a great success.

The façade of the church consists of a loggia and a portico (by Francis Tasker in 1891) with two arches, above which are three alcoves, containing a statue of Christ in the centre with statues of St Bede and St George either side. Between the alcoves are two large mosaics depicting the miracle of the fishes and Jesus giving the keys of the Kingdom of Heaven to St Peter. Above the façade is a 108-ft (33m) bell tower built in 1891, housing a huge bell known as 'The Steel Monster'. Looking up from the central nave, the ceiling is dominated by a fresco depicting St Peter in triumph, carrying symbols of his authority and martyrdom (Gauthier of Saluzzo, 1896).

> A memorial plaque inside the loggia commemorates the sinking of the S.S. Arandora Star, torpedoed by a German U-boat on 2nd July 1940 while transporting German and Italian civilian internees and POWs from Liverpool to Canada, with the loss of over 800 lives, including 446 Italians.

The choir loggia and organ were built in 1886. Today's magnificent organ is part of the original by the Belgian craftsman Anneesen and was regarded as the finest in the country at the time of its installation. Maintaining the tradition of fine singing at St Peter's, it has accompanied many exceptional vocalists, including the great tenor, Beniamino Gigli.

Address: 37a Clerkenwell Green, EC1R 0DU (020-7253 1485, marx-memorial-library.org.uk)

Opening hours: Mon-Thu noon-4pm or by appointment

Cost: free

Transport: Farringdon tube

Karl Heinrich Marx

MARX MEMORIAL LIBRARY

Housed in a Grade II listed building, the Marx Memorial Library is dedicated to the advancement of education, knowledge and learning through books, periodicals and manuscripts relating to all aspects of the science of Marxism, the history of Socialism and the working class movement. Since its establishment it has been the intellectual home of generations of scholars interested in studying Marx and Marxism. The Library contains an impressive number and variety of archives and collections, including the full run of the *Daily Worker* and *Morning Star* newspapers, the International Brigade Archive, the Bernal Peace Library, the Klugmann Collection and an extensive Photograph Library.

Karl Heinrich Marx (1818-1883) was a German philosopher, sociologist, economic historian, journalist and revolutionary socialist who developed the socio-political theory of Marxism. His ideas have since played a significant role in the development of social science and the socialist political movement. He published various books, the most notable being *The Communist Manifesto* (1848) and *Capital* (1867-1894), many co-written with his friend and fellow German revolutionary socialist, Friedrich Engels (1820-1895). Marx moved to London in May 1849 and remained in the city until dying as a stateless person on 14th March 1883. He's buried in Highgate Cemetery.

The building housing the Library was built in 1738 as a Welsh charity school for boys who were the children of Welsh artisans living in poverty in Clerkenwell. When

Lenin was exiled in London and worked in the building from April 1902 to May 1903 – his office is preserved and open to visitors.

the intake became too large the school moved to new premises in 1772 and the building was used as workshops. The Twentieth Century Press occupied the building in 1909, founded by the Social Democratic Federation as the printer of its journal, *Justice*. During its time in Clerkenwell Green, the Press produced several of the earliest English editions of Marx's and Engels's works.

In 1933, on the 50th anniversary of Marx's death, a meeting comprising trades unionists and veteran socialists belonging to the Labour and Communist Parties considered erecting a permanent memorial to him, and resolved that a library would be the most appropriate. Thus the *Marx Memorial Library & Workers' School* (as it was then known) was established. Study classes, held in the evenings, became the distinguishing feature of the Workers' School, which was divided into faculties of science, history and political economy. The Library expanded to occupy the whole building over the years.

Duke of Gloucester

MUSEUM OF THE ORDER OF ST JOHN

The Museum of the Order of St John tells the unique and fascinating story of the Order of the Hospital of St John of Jerusalem, founded after the first Crusade captured Jerusalem in 1099. It occupies two sites in Clerkenwell: St John's Gate (1504), the entrance to the former Priory of the Knights of St John, and the Priory Church of St John, Clerkenwell, with its surviving 12th-century crypt. The Museum's diverse collections explore all aspects of the Order's history and include rare illuminated manuscripts (such as the Rhodes Missal of 1504), armour, weapons, paintings, coins, furnishings, ceramics, silverware and textiles, plus historic first-aid equipment and memorabilia from St John's role in the two world wars.

The story spans over 900 years and includes many key events and people. Beginning with the Crusades, and continuing through revolts and revolutions, war and peace, it traverses the centuries and shows how warrior monks set out from the priory in Clerkenwell to fight for the faith and tend the sick.

The Order originally consisted of a group of Knights – men from noble European families who took vows of poverty, chastity, obedience and care of the sick. Later it took on a military role and took control of Crusader castles. When Palestine was recaptured by Muslim forces in 1291, the Order moved briefly to Cyprus and then, in 1309, to Rhodes. When the Turkish Sultan, Suleiman the Magnificent, conquered the island in 1522, the Order moved to Malta. After a famous siege by Suleiman in 1565, which the Knights and the Maltese people survived, a new capital city, Valetta, was built. The Order's ships patrolled the Mediterranean and remained on Malta until 1798, when the island was lost to Napoleon.

> Men, money and supplies were sent from the priory to hospitals – including one founded to care for sick pilgrims in 11th-century Jerusalem – on the great medieval pilgrim routes.

The original Roman Catholic Order still has its headquarters in Rome, its full title being 'The Sovereign Military Hospitaller Order of St John of Jerusalem, of Rhodes and of Malta.' It remains a sovereign entity in international law and is engaged in international charity work. St John has maintained its caring role to this day, working worldwide on numerous humanitarian projects. Victorian pioneers began a first-aid movement that spread around the globe and continues today with St John Ambulance and the St John Eye Hospital in Jerusalem.

AT A GLANCE

Address: **1 Scala Street, W1T 2HL (020-7636 3452, pollockstoys.com)**
Opening hours: **Mon-Sat 10am-5pm, closed Sun and bank holidays**
Cost: **adults £7, seniors/students £6, children £4**
Transport: **Goodge Street tube**

POLLOCK'S TOY MUSEUM

Pollock's Toy Museum is home to a fascinating collection of toy theatres, teddy bears, wax and china dolls, board games, optical toys, folk toys, nursery furniture, mechanical toys and doll's houses. It takes its name from Benjamin Pollock (1856-1937), the last of the Victorian Toy Theatre printers. Pollock, a simple, modest man, achieved considerable fame and became a legend in his own lifetime. Despite his fame, he remained in his birthplace of Hoxton (Hackney), where he devoted his life to his pokey little shop, and by his diligence kept going for 60 years. His passing didn't go unnoticed, however, and earned him an obituary of eight column inches in *The Times*.

The Toy Museum was established by Marguerite Fawdry (1912-1995), who in 1954 wanted some wire slides for her son's toy theatre, and found the business closed (after the owner went bankrupt). Following enquiries, she was told by a weary accountant: 'I believe there are hundreds of thousands in the warehouse, madam, but there's no one who can look them out for you... Of course you could, I suppose, buy the lot if you wanted them.' And so Fawdry bought up the entire stock of Benjamin Pollock Ltd. – and a museum was born.

The Toy Museum was established in 1956 in a single attic room at 44 Monmouth Street, near Covent Garden, and as the shop and museum grew other rooms were annexed. By 1969 the business had outgrown its premises and moved to Scala Street. It has now been a family owned and run business for three generations.

Pollock's is an active producer of toy theatres and has a large collection of toy theatre production items, printing plates, theatres, printed sheets

> 'If you love art, folly, or the bright eyes of children, speed to Pollock's.'
>
> Robert Louis Stevenson (1880s).

of scenes and characters, and general toy theatre paraphernalia (with over 100 toy theatres in its collection). Nearly every kind of toy imaginable turns up here from all over the world and from all different time periods.

Today the museum occupies two connected 18th-century residential houses with original period fire places, windows and doors, and rooms connected by narrow winding staircases. The whole place exudes atmosphere and evocations of those special times of childhood, with every corner filled with visual delights.

There's a Benjamin Pollock's Toyshop in Covent Garden (44 The Market), which opened in 1980, although nowadays it's only connected to the museum by its shared history, having parted ways in 1988.

AT A GLANCE

Address: **14 Ely Place, EC1N 6RY (020-7405 1061, stetheldreda.com)**

Opening hours: **Mon-Sat 8am-5pm, Sun 8am-12.30pm. See website for service times.**

Cost: **free**

Transport: **Chancery Lane or Farringdon tube**

ST ETHELDREDA'S CHURCH

uilt around 1250 by John De Kirkeby (d 1290), Bishop of Ely and Treasurer of England, St Etheldreda's is the oldest Roman Catholic church in England and one of only two surviving buildings in London from the reign of Edward I. Originally the town chapel of the Bishops of Ely (1250-1570), Ely Place was once one of the most influential places in London, with a palace and vast grounds, while its chapel took its name from one of England's most popular saints.

Princess Etheldreda, daughter of King Anna, a prominent member of the ruling family of the Kingdom of East Anglia, was born in 630. She wanted to be a nun but agreed to a political marriage with a neighbouring king, Egfrith, on condition that she could remain a virgin. When the king tried to break the agreement she fled to Ely, where she founded a religious community and built a magnificent church on the ruins of one founded by St Augustine. After her death in 679, devotion to her spread rapidly and later, through popular demand, she was moved to a more fitting tomb, which led to the (alleged) discovery that after 15 years in wet earth her body was in a perfect state of preservation.

St Etheldreda's Church miraculously survived the Great Fire in 1666 but deteriorated over the next few hundred years – during which it served as a prison, a hospital and even a tavern! – until becoming a Catholic (Rosminian – see rosmini.org) church in 1874. The church was badly damaged in World War Two and wasn't fully repaired until 1952. Today its walls are inset with statues of martyrs and there are some beautiful examples of stained glass; the great west window – reputedly the largest in London – was made in 1952 by Joseph Edward Nuttgens (1892-1982) and reflects the medieval splendour of the original. The church also has a beautiful cloister garden.

> The thoroughfare known as Ely Place (1775) is unique in several respects: the gate is closed at 10pm and until 1939 a nightwatchman toured the cul-de-sac calling out the hours.

Although just a stone's throw from the noise and bustle of 21st-century London, amid the clamour of mammon, St Etheldreda's is a hidden gem; a spiritual sanctuary of the Middle Ages and a haven of peace and tranquillity. The interior conveys a real sense of age and mystery. A visit to this beautiful church is a real treat – go on a Sunday morning to catch one of the regular choral recitals.

Address: **21 Stacey Street, WC2H 8DG (thephoenixgarden.org)**
Opening hours: **Mon-Fri 10am-dusk, weekends dawn-dusk**
Cost: **free**
Transport: **Tottenham Court Road, Leicester Square or Covent Garden tube**

PHOENIX GARDEN

This little oasis is next to the Phoenix Theatre and is the last remaining of Covent Garden's seven community gardens, and one of the West End's best kept secrets. Founded in 1984, it's maintained by volunteers and funded entirely by donations, having risen, Phoenix-like, from the ashes. Built on the site of the old St Giles Leper Hospital (established by Queen Maud) which existed from 1117-1539, the award-winning garden's location has an interesting history, having been the site of a charity school, a tragic World War Two bombing and a car park.

The location's green-fingered connections date back to the 17th century, when a local gardener called Brown rented space in the nearby St Giles-in-the-Fields churchyard, giving rise to Brown's Gardens (the name by which Stacey Street was originally known). Centuries later its less-than-ideal growing conditions have proved no obstacle to the flourishing display of flowers, grasses, shrubs and trees (including rowan, willow, walnut, birch and ginkgo) that you see today. There's also a rockery and a small fish pond, benches (with quirky inscriptions) and a children's play area – it's very much a living garden with a real heart and soul.

Here innovation and environmentally-sound thinking go hand in hand, as the retaining walls, made from recycled newspapers, and its Gabion dry stone wall constructed from excavated bomb rubble illustrate. The garden is maintained using sustainable techniques and an innovative approach to wildlife gardening, with

In conjunction with St Giles-in-the-Fields, the garden plays host to regular community events such as an annual agricultural 'Country Show', which showcases locally grown plants and produce, Morris dancing and other traditional entertainments, including a Punch and Judy show and falconry displays.

plants that grow reliably in dry conditions, look good year-round and are of maximum benefit to wildlife. It's become a haven for city wildlife, including five species of bee, butterflies and a variety of birds such as the blue and great tit, robin, wren, house sparrow, blackbird, greenfinch, sparrow hawk, woodpecker and kestrel. It's also home to the West End's only frogs, which inhabit its ponds along with colourful damselflies.

The garden was under threat of closure in 2015 (its lease was eventually renewed for 20 years), when it closed for an 18-month renovation, during which an event space building was constructed.

So, when you're tired of tramping the West End streets and your batteries need recharging, make a beeline for this peaceful haven, relax, read a book, have a nap or a spot of lunch, smell the roses or simply watch the clouds drift by.

Address: 60 Great Queen Street, WC2B 5AZ (020-7395 9257, museumfreemasonry.org.uk)

Opening hours: Mon-Sat 10am-5pm, closed Sun. The museum also organises free guided tours (Mon-Sat, up to five a day at 11am, noon, 2pm, 3pm and 4pm) of the Grand Temple and ceremonial areas. Sat tours must be pre-booked.

Cost: free

Transport: Holborn or Covent Garden tube

FREEMASONS' HALL & MUSEUM OF FREEMASONRY

Freemasons' Hall has been the centre of English Freemasonry for over 230 years. It's the headquarters of the United Grand Lodge of England, the oldest Grand Lodge in the world, and also the meeting place for over 1,000 Masonic lodges. The present building, the third Masonic Hall on the site, was built as a memorial to those who died in World War One, and was for many years known as the Masonic Peace Memorial. The Art Deco building (Grade II* listed), designed by H. V. Ashley and F. Winton Newman and completed in 1933, covers two acres; it forms an irregular hollow pentagram with the Grand Temple in the centre and adopts a diagonal axis to cope with the awkward shape of the site.

The building is constructed on a steel frame and faced with Portland stone. The principal ceremonial rooms are situated on the first floor where three vestibules form a ceremonial approach to the Grand Temple and are of increasing richness in architectural treatment and design. In the second vestibule there are displays about Freemasonry and the history of the site and the building. The first vestibule lies above the ceremonial entrance to the building, below the tower at the junction of Great Queen Street and Wild Street. The stained-glass windows on either side represent the six days of the creation. On one side these are shown with the five orders of architecture and on the other with five Masonic symbols. The beautiful shrine was designed by Walter Gilbert (1871-1946).

> The Museum contains an extensive collection of Masonic objects, including pottery and porcelain, glassware, silver, furniture, clocks, jewels and regalia.

Items belonging to famous and royal Freemasons, including Winston Churchill and Edward VII, are displayed together with examples from the Museum's extensive collection of prints and engravings, photographs and ephemera. The collection explores the different ranks, offices and branches of Freemasonry and also explains some of the symbolism used, the charities established, Masonic dining habits, as well as Freemasonry abroad and during wartime. There's also a large collection of items relating to non-Masonic fraternal societies, such as the Oddfellows and the Sons of the Phoenix.

The Library is open for reference use and contains one of the leading collections of Masonic artefacts, books and manuscripts. These cover every facet of Freemasonry in England, as well as material on Freemasonry elsewhere in the world and on subjects associated with Freemasonry or with mystical and esoteric traditions.

AT A GLANCE

Address: 15-20 Phoenix Place, WC1X 0DA (0300-0300 700, postalmuseum.org)

Opening hours: 10am-5pm

Cost: adults £17, 16-24s £12, children (under 16) £10 (£1 saving when booked online); tickets are valid for one year

Transport: Russell Square tube

POSTAL MUSEUM & MAIL RAIL

The Postal Museum began life as the British Postal Museum & Archive in 2004 and was renamed the Postal Museum in 2016 and opened in 2017 in Clerkenwell, within the formal mail rail terminal for the Mount Pleasant Mail Centre. The museum brings five centuries of communications history to life and reveals the fascinating story of Britain's postal heritage through its extraordinary collections. From interactive galleries to an immersive subterranean rail ride, modern research facilities to a wide-range of learning activities, the museum offers something for everyone. The museum's attractions include a commemorative stamp that would have been used had Scotland won the 1976 FIFA World Cup (the ultimate wishful thinking!), telegrams from the night that the *Titanic* sank, and the original copy of *Ulysses.*

One of the highlights of the new museum is a ride on London's Mail Rail, the world's first driverless electric railway constructed by John Mowlem & Co 1915-1927. The Post Office Railway, known as Mail Rail since 1987, is a 2ft (610 mm) narrow gauge, driverless underground railway built to move mail between the city's sorting offices. Inspired by the Chicago Tunnel Company, who built a similar railway under the streets of Chicago in 1906, the railway operated from 1927 until 2003. The line ran from the Paddington Head District Sorting Office in the west to the Eastern Head District Sorting Office at Whitechapel in the east, a distance of 6½ miles (10½ km). It had eight stations, the largest of which was beneath Mount Pleasant, but by 2003 (when the railway closed) only three stations remained in use.

Today you can take a 15-minute journey on the miniature train under the streets of London through the original tunnels and largely unchanged station platforms of

> The first National Postal Museum (NPM) was established in 1966, in part due to the Phillips Collection of Victorian philately donated to the nation by Reginald M. Philips. The museum was opened in 1969 and included a collection of postal equipment, uniforms, vehicles and more – far more than could be displayed in the small museum. The museum closed in 1998 and the management of the museum and post office archive were combined.

the 100-year-old postal railway. The railway exhibition allows you to see and hear the people who worked on the railway, experience their lives below ground and glimpse hidden parts of the railway that once kept the mail coursing through London for 22 hours every day.

1. Hackney Empire
2. St Mary's Secret Garden
3. Victoria Park
4. Tower Hamlets Cemetery Park
5. Old Spitalfields Market
6. Christ Church Spitalfields
7. Brick Lane & Markets
8. Royal London Hospital Museum
9. Cable Street Mural
10. The Grapes

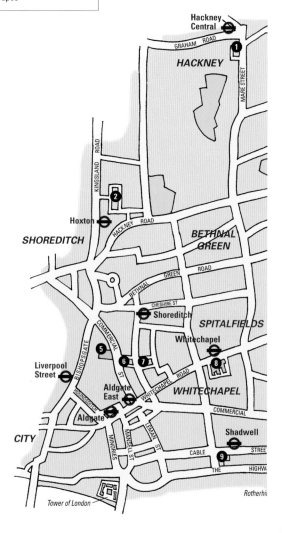

EAST LONDON

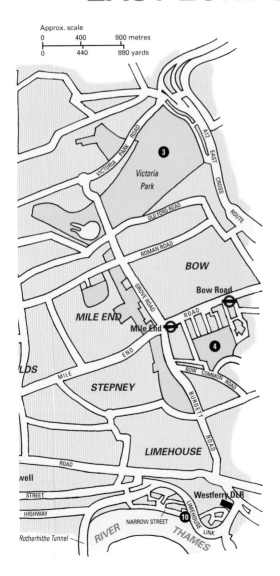

HACKNEY EMPIRE

Built in 1901, the Hackney Empire (Grade II* listed) with its electric lights, central heating and in-built projection box, was a technological wonder of its time, designed by the great Frank Matcham (1854-1920), one of the world's most accomplished and inventive theatre architects.

When the theatre opened under the ownership of Sir Oswald Stoll (1866-1942) it attracted acts from all over the world. Chaplin appeared a number of times before decamping to America to gain fame in Hollywood, and Stan Laurel perfected his act here. However, the most important star to appear in this heyday of music hall before World War One was Marie Lloyd – who lived in Graham Road close to the theatre – whose act consciously shocked and challenged her audiences. This 'Queen of the Halls' lent her support to an artists' strike in 1907 which led to the formation of the Variety Artists' Association, now part of the actors' union, Equity.

Between the wars the Empire hosted burlesque, reviews, plays and concerts, as well as variety – even Louis Armstrong was enticed from Harlem to appear here. In the years after World War Two audiences flocked to see artists made household names by the radio, such as Charlie Chester, Issy Bonn, Tony Hancock – and even Liberace! The Empire continued as a centre of popular culture until 1956, when it was sold to ATV and became the country's first commercial TV studios, where programmes such as *Take Your Pick*, *Oh Boy!* (the *Top Of The Pops* of its day) and *Emergency Ward 10* were filmed.

> By 2001, the Empire's centenary year, the theatre had raised £17 million to fund its restoration and modernisation; it reopened in January 2004 with a café/bar.

In 1963, the Empire reached its nadir when Mecca purchased it and converted it into a bingo hall. Its saving grace came when the building was listed in 1984 and Mecca sold up rather than restore the Mare Street façade. It was revived by C.A.S.T. (Cartoon Archetypical Slogan Theatre), a satirical touring theatre group, as a permanent base and to resurrect it as a venue for popular theatre. It reopened on its 85th birthday, 9 December 1986, and was soon established as one of the country's leading stand-up comedy venues, where many of today's stars got their first break.

The grand old dame still has them rolling in the aisles after almost 120 years, presenting a mixture of variety, comedy, drama, dance, opera and pantomime – long may it continue.

AT A GLANCE

Address: 50 Pearson Street, E2 8EL (020-7739 2965, stmaryssecretgarden.org.uk)

Opening hours: Mon-Fri 9am-5pm, usually closed weekends. Tours can be arranged.

Cost: **free**

Transport: **Hoxton rail**

ST MARY'S SECRET GARDEN

St Mary's Secret Garden is named after St Mary's Church Haggerston, which was situated nearby but was destroyed in World War Two. Designed by John Nash (1752-1835), the church was built in 1827 and its churchyard later laid out as a public garden by the Earl and Countess of Meath in 1882. The current garden was created when the World War Two pre-fabs (which replaced Georgian terraces) were demolished in the '70s and the area was designated a community space – an old street lamp within the garden recalls the previous street that ran through the site.

In the '90s local residents established a community garden here, which was run as a therapeutic garden project by Thrive until 2003, when it was renamed St Mary's Secret Garden. Today it remains a community garden with the emphasis on social and therapeutic gardening. This small sanctuary – just 0.7acre/0.28ha – is an oasis in the middle of a busy area of the capital. It's divided into four areas: a natural woodland section with a pond, a food growing area (including vegetable beds, soft fruit and fruit trees), a herb and sensory garden and an area of herbaceous borders. It also has a classroom and large greenhouse. Organic principles are used in maintaining the garden and to encourage wildlife and biodiversity.

The garden offers horticultural therapy and training for those with mental health issues, terminal illnesses, learning and physical disabilities and other health problems, to

> St Mary's provides a wide range of projects including accredited horticultural education (basic gardening courses, herbal workshops, plus teachers' gardening with children); outreach work to other organisations; planting workshops at festivals and events; work experience for students and school children; community events such as an annual flower show; and plant, fruit and vegetable sales.

enhance their physical and mental well-being. It also provides the opportunity for individuals to complete meaningful tasks which contribute to the running and maintenance of the garden. Placements, volunteering and training opportunities are provided for Hackney's diverse community, and therapists work with individuals and community groups, including young offenders and those with HIV.

St Mary's is very much a community garden and is available for local families and groups to use through a keyholder scheme. Visitors are welcome to enjoy the garden – a beautiful spot to savour a few minutes peace and quiet.

AT A GLANCE

Address: **Grove Road, E3 5TB (020-8985 5699,**
towerhamlets.gov.uk/lgnl/leisure_and_culture/parks_and_open_spaces/
victoria_park/victoria_park.aspx)
Opening hours: **daily 7am-dusk**
Cost: **free**
Transport: **Mile End tube**

VICTORIA PARK

Victoria Park – known colloquially as 'Vicky Park' – is a beautiful space extending to 218 acres (86ha) bordering parts of Bethnal Green, Hackney and Bow (situated entirely within the borough of Tower Hamlets, which manages the park). Today it's a key link in a green corridor stretching from the Thames at Limehouse, along the Regents Canal and through Mile End Park.

Opened in 1845, Victoria Park is the oldest public park (Grade II listed) in Britain built specifically for the people – hence its nickname of the 'people's park'. It remains at the heart of east London life today and has long been a centre for political meetings and rallies, perhaps exceeding in importance the better-known Hyde Park in this regard.

The need for a park in the East End of London became apparent when the population grew rapidly in the early 19th century due to the development of the docks and industry. This resulted in overcrowded housing, leading to poor health and low life expectancy. The first official acknowledgment of the situation came in the 1839 annual report of the Registrar General of Births, Deaths and Marriages, which showed a mortality rate far higher than for the rest of London, due to massive overcrowding, insanitary conditions and polluted air.

> The park contains a number of unusual features, including a pair of stone alcoves (with seating) from the old London Bridge (demolished in 1831), a highly decorated drinking fountain and two stone sculptures, the 'Dogs of Alcibiades' (at the entrance).

Victoria Park was created as a place for people to breathe clean air and it also became a place of horticultural excellence. It still boasts some delightful open parkland with a variety of shrubs and trees, wide tree-lined carriageways, deer park, lakes, leisure gardens and ornate bridges over canal-ways; it's a stunning example of a formal Victorian London park, reminiscent of Regent's Park.

Victoria Park hosts a wide range of formal and informal sports, sponsored activities, events, festivals and music concerts, throughout the year. It's also great for children and has herds of deer and goats, a programme of summer activities, and an excellent children's play park with a paddling pool.

In 2011, the park underwent a £12 million refurbishment, including the creation of a Chinese pagoda in the West Lake, a new community facility and café, and the building of two new play areas. The park has an excellent café (Pavilion Café) overlooking the boating lake, which specialises in serving breakfast /brunch.

Address: **Southern Grove, E3 4PX** (020-8983 1277, towerhamlets.gov.uk/
lgnl/leisure_and_culture/parks_and_open_spaces/cemetery_park.aspx,
fothcp.org)

Opening hours: **dawn to dusk (via the main gates). Free guided walk (2
hours) at 2pm on the third Sun of the month (see fothcp.org)**

Cost: **free**

Transport: **Mile End or Bow Road tube**

TOWER HAMLETS CEMETERY PARK

Tower Hamlets Cemetery Park (known locally as Bow Cemetery) is a historic cemetery opened in 1841 – the last and least known of London's Magnificent Seven Cemeteries created in the 1830s and 1840s to solve the city's chronic shortage of burial grounds. It was the most working class of the cemeteries and during its first two years 60 per cent of burials were in public graves for those who couldn't afford a plot and funeral (which increased to 80 per cent by 1851).

The cemetery became neglected over the years, which led to it being purchased by the Greater London Council in 1966 and closed to burials in order to create a public park in the heart of this intensively built-up area. In 1986, ownership was passed to the borough of Tower Hamlets and in 1990 the Friends of the Tower Hamlets Cemetery Park was created. The cemetery became Tower Hamlets' first local nature reserve in 2001 and is managed and maintained by the Friends.

The park covers an area of 33 acres (13.4ha) of mature broadleaved woodland and meadow, with an outstanding variety of wild plants, flowers and animals. The wildlife includes over 20 butterfly species and around 40 bird species, which can be heard on the annual International Dawn Chorus Day walk (usually 1st May). Parts of the park are managed wilderness, while others, particularly the two pond areas, are used for teaching environmental science to local school children, who use it as an outdoor classroom.

In 2002, the Cantrell Road Maze was created in scrapyard meadows – the name indicates its former use – where Friends and local volunteers made a chalk maze based on a classical design. A green corridor link – the Ackroyd Drive Greenlink – has also been created between the Cemetery Park and Mile End Park.

The high brick walls surrounding the cemetery are Grade II listed, as are 16 individual grave memorials – there are some fascinating memorial stones, particularly of angels. Today the park is a wonderful, if slightly spooky, green space, and has been designated a conservation area, a Local Nature Reserve and a Site of Metropolitan Importance for Nature Conservation. It's a wonderful place to relax and forget the stresses of the modern world.

> People entirely unrelated to each other would be buried in the same grave within the space of a few weeks, and there were stories of some graves being 40 feet deep and containing up to 30 bodies.

Address: **16 Horner Square, E1 6EW (020-7377 1496, spitalfields.co.uk and oldspitalfieldsmarket.com)**

Opening hours: **Mon-Wed, Fri 10am-8pm, Thu 7am-6pm, Sat 10am-6pm, Sun 10am-5pm (check individual shops/stalls for opening hours)**

Cost: **free**

Transport: **Liverpool Street or Aldgate tube**

OLD SPITALFIELDS MARKET

Old Spitalfields Market is one of London's finest surviving Victorian market halls, located just outside the City in Spitalfields. The area is something of a 'hidden gem', famous not only for its handful of cobbled streets of Georgian houses, but also for its contemporary apartments, many converted from soup kitchens, Victorian baths and old tannery warehouses.

There's been a market on the site since 1638, when Charles I granted a licence for 'flesh, fowl and roots' to be sold on Spittle Fields, then a rural area on the outskirts of London. The existing buildings were built in 1887 to service a wholesale fruit and vegetable market, which moved to Leyton in 1991 (the New Spitalfields Market). The original Victorian market buildings and the market hall and roof were restored – now resplendent under a Fosters & Partners-designed glass canopy – and offer a fusion of Victorian splendour and cutting-edge contemporary architecture.

Nestled in the shadow of Christ Church (see next page), the market offers the perfect antidote to out-of-town shopping malls, and is a popular fashion, food, vintage and general market open seven days a week. Escape from the cloned high streets and discover unique retailers, from fashion and arts to interiors and antiques, as you wander through an area steeped in history, now a centre of creativity and style. Spitalfields Market is surrounded by independent shops, cafés, bars and awarding-winning restaurants such as the Wright Bros seafood restaurant, Michelin-starred La Chapelle and Blixen, a gorgeous restaurant (all-day dining) in the style of a European grand café.

> The market also offers regular free events, including lunchtime concerts, festivals, tango classes, fashion shows and much more.

Although the market is open seven days a week, the busiest days are Thursdays to Sundays (Sundays are the most popular). From Mondays to Wednesdays there's a general (Daily) market offering fashion, footwear, gifts and bric-a-brac. On Thursdays, the antiques market attracts tourists, dealers and collectors on the lookout for bargains, while on Fridays it's the destination of fashion fans and art lovers, with a wealth of innovative design (joined by the Vinyl Market on the first and third Friday of the month). On Saturdays there's a mixture of fashion (Style Market – both vintage and new), art, jewellery, crafts and fair trade products, plus antiques and collectibles, while on Sundays stallholders traditionally sell a bit of everything, from (organic) food to fashion, furniture to art – with something for everyone.

After you've shopped till you drop, chill out with a coffee, glass of wine or a meal in one of the many excellent restaurants and cafés.

CHRIST CHURCH SPITALFIELDS

Lovely 18th-century Christ Church Spitalfields is off the usual tourist track, although its locale of Spitalfields is becoming more popular with the discerning visitor. The church was designed by Nicholas Hawksmoor (1661-1736), a pupil of Sir Christopher Wren and one of England's foremost architects. It was built between 1714 and 1729 as part of the church building programme initiated by the Fifty New Churches act of 1711 (only 12 of which were completed, six by Hawksmoor), to cater for the 'godless thousands' outside the City of London who had no adequate church provision.

Noted for the eloquence of its beautiful stonework and pleasing geometry, Christ Church is the size of a small cathedral and inside it's the height of Exeter Cathedral, with a volume half that of the nave of St Paul's. Its architectural composition demonstrates Hawksmoor's usual abruptness: the plain rectangular box of the nave is surmounted at its west end by a broad tower of three stages, topped by a steeple more Gothic than classical (the magnificent porch was a later addition).

Inside, large glass-paned doors lead from the vestibule into the nave, an oak-panelled hall with Purbeck stone floor and a ceiling of flowers, each one unique. Lit by chandeliers, this grand space has been lovingly restored to retain its authentic 18th-century charm. Hawksmoor's bold symmetrical design displays the ornate ceiling perfectly, while the huge columns provide natural divisions, giving the room a unique versatility. Above the nave on either side are galleries.

The church has seen at least two large-scale renovations, the first in 1866 (directed by the architect Ewan Christian), which 'savagely' changed the entire look of the interior, and the second which began in the '60s when the church was derelict. The latter restoration – to its original state, following the ill-advised changes wrought by Christian – was only completed in 2004 at a cost of £10 million (the estimate was £1 million!). The restoration is a revelation and has revealed one of the most complex and sumptuous of Hawksmoor's interiors. There's also a café – Café in the Crypt – open Mon-Sat 10am-4pm.

> Just as Christ Church is the masterpiece of its architect, the organ installed in 1735 was the masterpiece of the greatest organ builder in Georgian England, Richard Bridge (d 1758). It's the only remaining Bridge organ and bears witness to the vibrant and rich musical life of Georgian London.

BRICK LANE & MARKETS

Brick Lane is a street in Tower Hamlets which runs from Swanfield Street in Bethnal Green to Whitechapel High Street in the south by the short stretch of Osborn Street. Today it's the heart of the Bangladeshi-Sylheti community – known to some as *Banglatown* – noted for its numerous curry houses, although this is only one of its many claims to fame.

It derives its name from former brick and tile manufacturers dating to the 15th century. From the 17th century it was home to successive waves of immigrants, beginning with Huguenot refugees spreading from Spitalfields, followed by Irish, Ashkenazi Jews and, in the 20th century, Bangladeshis. The area became a centre for weaving, tailoring and the clothing industry, due to the abundance of semi- and unskilled immigrant labour. It continues to be a microcosm of London's shifting ethnic patterns and was once associated with poor slums and the notorious Jack the Ripper murders in 1888.

Brewing came to Brick Lane in the 17th century with Joseph Truman, first recorded in 1683. His family, particularly Benjamin Truman (1699-1780), established the Black Eagle Brewery (Grade II listed) at 91 Brick Lane, the largest in London, covering 11 acres (4.5ha). The brewery closed in 1988 and is now a vibrant arts and events centre, housing over 250 businesses, ranging from cultural venues and art galleries to bars, restaurants and shops (see trumanbrewery.com). Since the late '90s the Brewery has been the site of several of the East End's best night clubs, notably 93 Feet East and Café 1001. It's also home to two indoor weekly markets: the Backyard (Saturday/Sunday) and the Sunday UpMarket.

Brick Lane Market is a chaotic, colourful, artistic hub, attracting hordes of young people in search of second-hand furniture, unusual clothes, jewellery, arts and crafts, bric-a-brac and food. Go on a Sunday to catch it at its best. The joy is that you never know what you'll find; anything from cheap leather and vintage clothes to old magazines and kitsch collectibles, stunning silks to period furniture.

> Street performers enhance the vibrant, lively atmosphere, while Brick Lane is also famous for its graffiti, featuring artists such as Banksy, D'Face and Ben Eine.

After you've had your fill of shopping, enjoy a coffee and bagels (try Beigel Bake at number 159) or an inexpensive lunch in one of the many authentic Bangladeshi restaurants.

AT A GLANCE

Address: Royal London Hospital, St Augustine with St Philip's Church, Newark Street, E1 2AA (020-7377 7608, museumslondon.org/museum/141/royal-london-hospital-museum)

Opening hours: Tue-Fri 10am-12.20pm, 1-4pm

Cost: free

Transport: Whitechapel tube

Edith Cavell

Joseph Merrick (Elephant Man)

ROYAL LONDON HOSPITAL MUSEUM

This museum is (appealingly) located in the former crypt of St Philip's Church, a fine, late 19th-century church, designed by Arthur Cawston. It tells the story of the hospital (founded 1740), originally named the London Infirmary, which changed to the London Hospital in 1748 and then to the Royal London Hospital on its 250th anniversary in 1990. The museum reopened to the public in 2002 following a major refurbishment and also accommodates the library of the School of Medicine and Dentistry at Whitechapel. Visitors wishing to see the church can do so on weekdays, subject to the approval of the duty librarian.

The museum has revamped sections on the history of the hospital since its foundation in 1740, including those dedicated to Joseph Merrick (1862-1890 – the 'Elephant Man'), who spent his last years at the Royal London (his mounted skeleton is kept at the Medical School but isn't on public display).

A showcase on forensic medicine features original material on Dr Crippen, the Christie and Whitechapel ('Jack the Ripper') murders, and the London Hospital surgeon and curator, Thomas Horrocks Openshaw (1856-1929), who helped to investigate them. It also houses a permanent exhibition of artefacts and archives relating to the hospital and the history of healthcare in the East End, plus works of art, surgical instruments, medical and nursing equipment, uniforms, medals, and written archives containing documents dating back to 1740, including complete patient records since 1883.

The museum is arranged into three sections, covering the 18th, 19th and 20th centuries,

> The museum celebrates the lives of key figures such as surgeons Sir William Blizard (1743-1835) and Frederick Treves (1853-1923); hospital matron Eva Luckes (1854-1919), nurse Edith Cavell (1865-1915 – the war hero shot as a spy in World War One); and Dr Barnardo (1845-1905), the founder of homes for poor children.

with special sections on hospital uniforms, forensic medicine and dentistry, including a denture made for George Washington. Displays include original surgical instruments used in the era before antisepsis, forensic medicine, hospital uniforms and dentistry equipment.

The BBC TV series *Casualty 1906, 1907* and *1909* are set at the Royal London, and follow the everyday life of the hospital in these years, with some of the storylines based on actual cases drawn from the hospital records. But don't let that put you off: this fascinating museum is well worth a visit.

Address: 236 Cable Street, Tower Hamlets, E1 0BL (battleofcablestreet.org.uk)

Opening hours: unrestricted access

Cost: free

Transport: Shadwell DLR

CABLE STREET MURAL

The Cable Street Mural was painted to celebrate a 'victory' against fascism on 4th October 1936, when people in the East End of London stopped Oswald Mosley and his British Union of Fascists marching through Cable Street, then mainly a Jewish area. The ensuing clash became known as the 'Battle of Cable Street'. Despite the strong likelihood of violence, the government refused to ban the march and a large police escort was provided in an attempt to prevent anti-fascist protestors disrupting it. The anti-fascist groups (which included local Jewish, socialist, anarchist, Irish and communist organisations) erected roadblocks in an attempt to prevent the march from taking place. A slogan from the Spanish Civil War, a popular anti-fascist cause of the time, was widely used: '*No Pasaran!*' (they shall not pass!).

An estimated 250,000 anti-fascist demonstrators turned out, while over 10,000 police, including 4,000 on horseback, attempted to clear the road to allow the march to proceed. The demonstrators fought the police with sticks, rocks, chair legs and other improvised weapons, while rubbish, rotten vegetables and the contents of chamber pots were thrown by women from houses along the street. After a series of running battles, Mosley agreed to abandon the march to prevent bloodshed – and the fascists never actually clashed with the demonstrators. However, the anti-fascists continued to riot and 150 people were arrested. Over 100 people were injured, including policemen, women and children, and a number of policemen were kidnapped by demonstrators.

The Cable Street Mural commemorates this event and took a year to design and paint on the side of St

The disturbances led Parliament to pass the Public Order Act 1936, which empowered the police to ban demonstrations.

George's Town Hall, previously Stepney Town Hall and a local Vestry Hall. It was planned, researched and designed by artist Dave Binnington, who interviewed and included many local characters in the mural to illustrate the famous victory won by the East End people. However, it was completed (in 1982) by Ray Walker and Desmond Rochfort, Dave Binnington having quit after his early work was destroyed by vandals. The work was repeatedly defaced by fascists and members of the British Nationalist Party, both before and after it was completed, and has been repaired and renovated a number of times. Eventually a special varnish was applied so that future attacks could be easily cleaned off.

The mural stands as a powerful, symbolic reminder of anti-fascism in the East End.

Address: **76 Narrow Street, Limehouse, E14 8BP (020-7987 4396, thegrapes.co.uk)**

Opening hours: **Mon-Sat noon-11pm, Sun noon-10.30pm**

Cost: **free, except for the beer and food**

Transport: **Westferry DLR or Limehouse rail/DLR**

THE GRAPES

The Grade II listed Grapes is a delightful, tiny pub, built in 1720 – on the site of a previous pub dating to 1583 – when it was a working class tavern serving workers in the Limehouse Basin (which was a mass burial site for impoverished Londoners). Today it's a charming waterside pub, painted in bright blue with hanging baskets and window boxes, and elaborately etched windows. Standing at the end of a row of similar dwellings, it's a historic oasis in this now gentrified area, surrounded by ultra-modern buildings and luxury homes.

The Grapes has bags of character and a timeless East London atmosphere, with a cosy back room and an open fire in winter, friendly staff, free newspapers and board games (and no TV, fruit machines or juke boxes). One of the best features is the panoramic view of the Thames – provided you're fortunate enough to get one of the window seats in the Dickens' Snug. In summer, the small balcony is a lovely spot for a sheltered waterside drink, with easterly views towards Canary Wharf.

The Grapes serves good food and a choice of reasonably-priced real ales from the traditional Victorian long bar – it even has a dog-friendly bowl of water. Bar food (including whitebait, fish and chips, and steak & Guinness pie with garlic mash) is reasonably priced with good portions and roasts on Sundays. Upstairs is a highly-rated dining room specialising in fish dishes with a good wine list and panoramic views of the river.

Although tarted up and given a lick of paint, the Grapes remains pretty much as it was when Charles Dickens used it as a model for his Six Jolly Fellowship Porters in *Our Mutual Friend*. The pub was also a favourite of James Whistler, who used

> There are macabre stories of watermen snatching drunken patrons, drowning them in the river and selling their corpses for medical dissection – so take care when leaving!

it as the viewpoint for many of his river paintings, and Samuel Pepys records visiting lime kilns on the jetty. Historic Limehouse is also where Elizabethan explorer Sir Humphrey Gilbert lived and from where Sir Walter Raleigh set sail for the New World.

The pub changed hands in September 2011, the new leaseholder being none other than Sir Ian McKellen (Gandalf in the film, *Lord of the Rings*), who lives nearby – hopefully his 'magic' touch will ensure that the Grapes remains a mecca for pub fans.

1. Myddelton House Gardens
2. Forty Hall & Estate
3. Harrow School Tours & Museum
4. Golders Green Crematorium & Gardens
5. St Augustine's, Kilburn
6. Alexandra Palace & Park
7. Bruce Castle, Park & Museum
8. William Morris Gallery
9. Clissold Park & House

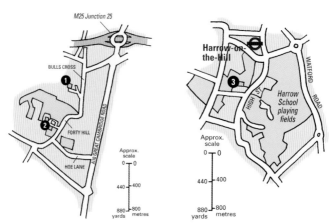

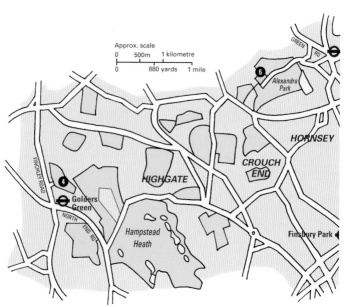

CHAPTER 6

NORTH LONDON

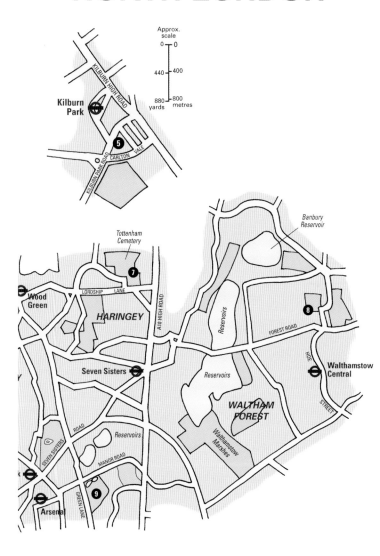

AT A GLANCE

Address: Bulls Cross, Enfield, EN2 9HG (0300-030610, leevalleypark.org. uk > nature, parks & gardens)

Opening hours: 10am-5pm or dusk if earlier; museum & tea room 10am-4pm

Cost: free; guided walks (1 hour) £5, minimum 15 people

Transport: Best reached by car via the M25, junction 25

MYDDELTON HOUSE GARDENS

Myddelton House was built by Henry Carrington Bowles (1763-1830) around 1818, replacing an earlier Elizabethan property, Bowling Green House. It was built in the then fashionable Suffolk white brick and named Myddelton House in honour of Sir Hugh Myddelton (1560-1631), an engineering genius who created the New River to supply London with fresh water, a section of which bisected the garden from 1613 until 1968.

When Bowles died in 1830 the house passed to his son (also Henry Bowles), who bequeathed it in 1852 to his nephew, Henry Carrington Bowles Treacher. He assumed the name Bowles in order to inherit the estate, thus becoming Henry Carrington Bowles Bowles! The garden was created by Henry's youngest son, E. A. (Edward Augustus or 'Gussie') Bowles (1865-1954), a renowned botanist, author, artist and Fellow of the Royal Horticultural Society – and one of the great gardeners of the 20th century. He originally trained for the church, but family tragedies caused him to change course and he remained at Myddelton House and developed the remarkable garden as a self-taught horticulturist. He became an expert on many plants, particularly snowdrops and crocuses, which earned him the sobriquet 'The Crocus King'.

Bowles never married and kept the house just as it was in his childhood. On his death, the house and gardens passed to the Royal Free Hospital School of Medicine and the London School of Pharmacy, which

> Secreted away near Enfield, this wonderful garden was neglected and forgotten for 30 years, hidden under layers of ivy and bramble.

grew a range of medicinal plants there. In 1967, the property was bought by the Lee Valley Regional Park Authority as its headquarters.

Myddelton House Gardens – restored to their former glory – cover an area of 6 acres (2.4ha) and offer an impressive range of flora and fauna. Within the Gardens are the national collection of award-winning bearded irises and 'special' areas which include the Lunatic Asylum (home to unusual plants), Tom Tiddler's Ground, Tulip Terrace, Alpine Meadow, Arboretum and the Kitchen Garden (created in 2002). The Gardens also have a beautiful carp pond, a Victorian conservatory, a rock garden, plus a number of historical artefacts collected by Bowles, including pieces from the original St Paul's Cathedral and the Enfield Market Cross.

The beautiful restored gardens contain a small visitor centre and tearoom and are an enchanting place to visit at any time of year.

FORTY HALL ESTATE

orty Hall (Grade I listed) and estate is Enfield 's 'Jewel in the Crown' and one of England's finest historic houses, built by former Lord Mayor of London, Sir Nicholas Rainton (1569-1646) in 1632. Situated at the edge of London, Forty Hall is important in understanding the growth of the city in the 17th century, and the life and times of the merchant classes who made London a major international trading centre.

When Sir Nicholas died in 1646, the Hall passed to his nephew, who extended the estate northwards by buying and demolishing neighbouring Elsyng (or Elsynge/Elsing) Palace in 1656. In 1894, the Hall was bought by Henry Carrington Bowles of neighbouring Myddelton House (see previous entry) for his son Major Henry Ferryman Bowles (1858-1943), MP for Enfield and later 1st Baronet Bowles. In 1951, the Bowles family sold the estate to the borough of Enfield, and since 1955 it has been open to the public and houses the borough's museum collection.

The Forty Hall Estate extends to 273 acres (110ha), containing a walled garden, formal and informal gardens, lakes, lawns, woodland, meadows and a farm. The estate parkland contains the rare archaeological remains of Elsyng Palace, a 14th-century Tudor hunting lodge used by Henry VIII and Elizabeth I. The Hall & Estate and the surrounding area of Forty Hill are a conservation area, with many superb buildings and a distinct historic village style.

The hall contains period furniture and furnishings along with collections of 17th- and 18th-century watercolours and drawings. The

> The Hall is important to historians as a fine example on the cusp between the medieval and modern styles. It has been changed and reworked by a string of owners over the centuries, but many architectural features remain from the 17th to 19th centuries. Today it has the external appearance of an 18th-century house.

wide-ranging museum collections focus on local and social history of the pre-1965 London boroughs of Edmonton, Southgate and Enfield (now the London Borough of Enfield), with the emphasis on everyday household ceramics and glass of the 19th and 20th centuries.

Forty Hall underwent a major restoration in 2011-12 (funded by the Heritage Lottery Fund) and features interpretation schemes telling the story of Sir Nicholas Rainton, education programmes, and an innovative events' programme focusing on art, ecology and heritage. A great day out for all the family.

AT A GLANCE

Address: 5 High Street, Harrow-on-the-Hill, HA1 3HP (020-8872 4638 for tours, harrowschool.org.uk)

Opening hours: Old Speech Room Gallery, 2.30-5pm on selected days (see website)

Cost: gallery free; open tours (2 hours) £6.50 per person. Also private guided tours.

Transport: Harrow-on-the-Hill tube

Lord Byron

Sir Winston Churchill

HARROW SCHOOL TOURS & GALLERY

Harrow School is an English independent school for boys founded in 1572 by John Lyon (d 1592) under a Royal Charter granted by Elizabeth I. The construction of the first school building began in 1608, after the death of Lyon's wife, and was completed in 1615. The original buildings remain, although the school is now much larger and covers an area of some 400 acres (160ha), including playing fields, tennis courts, golf course, woodland, gardens and its own working farm. The school isn't built on a campus, but is fully integrated into the surrounding area.

Harrow has an enrolment of around 850 boys, all full-time boarders in 12 boarding houses, each with its own facilities, customs and traditions, which compete in sporting events. Harrow has a rich history and many traditions, which include the boys' famous 'uniform' of boaters, morning suits, top hats and canes.

The school's long line of famous alumni includes eight former Prime Ministers (Churchill, Baldwin, Peel and Palmerston among them), numerous foreign statesmen, a number of kings and various other royals, 19 Victoria Cross holders and many leading figures in the arts and sciences, including Byron, Sheridan, Trollope, Dornford Yates, Richard Curtis, Lord Rayleigh, Fox Talbot, Sir Arthur Evans and Sir William Jones. It's widely considered one of the best secondary schools in the world, ranked alongside its famous rival Eton.

The Old Speech Room Gallery & Museum, located in the Old Speech Room built in 1819-1821 to encourage public speaking, was opened in 1976 to house the school's collections, which include Egyptian and Greek antiquities, English/European

> The school has its own unique form of 'dribbling' football, terminology and songs, which include Forty Years On – known as The Harrow Song – although it's one of many.

watercolours, modern British paintings, Japanese prints, books and natural history artefacts. The Museum hosts themed exhibitions from its collections. A number of musical events are held at the school during term-time to which members of the public are welcome, and many of the schools' sports facilities are available for hire.

Guided tours can be arranged on most weekdays in term-time or by arrangement during school holidays, when visitors can explore the Fourth Form Room, Old Speech Room Art Gallery, Speech Room, Chapel and Alex Fitch Room (among others). Open tours are also available, usually on Saturdays at 2pm (see website for details).

Address: Hoop Lane, Barnet, NW11 7NL (020-8455 2374;
thelondoncremation.co.uk/golders-green-crematorium)

Opening hours: 9am-6pm (summer), 9am-4pm (winter)

Cost: free

Transport: Golders Green tube

IN
LOVING
MEMORY
OF
MARC BOLAN
30.09.47 - 16.09.77
"25 YEARS ON HIS LIGHT OF
LOVE STILL SHINES BRIGHTLY"

PLACED BY THE OFFICIAL
MARC BOLAN FAN CLUB AND
FELLOW FANS TO COMMEMORATE
THE 25TH ANNIVERSARY
OF HIS PASSING

SEPTEMBER 2002

GOLDERS GREEN CREMATORIUM & GARDENS

Far from being morbid, Golders Green Crematorium is an inspiring and fascinating place to visit. It was London's first crematorium (opened in 1902) – and is one of the oldest in Britain – and was designed by Sir Ernest George (1839-1922), while the gardens were laid out by William Robinson (1838-1935). The crematorium is a red-brick building in Lombardic style which was constructed in stages as funds became available. The crematorium was completed around 1939, although some buildings have been added since, including three columbaria containing the ashes of thousands of Londoners.

The crematorium is secular, accepting all faiths and non-believers; clients may arrange their own type of service or remembrance event and choose whatever music they wish. Since 1902 over 300,000 cremations have taken place – far more than at any other British crematorium – and now average around 2,000 a year. (The first crematorium in Britain was established in Woking in 1878, although cremation wasn't legalised until 1884, with the first cremation taking place in 1885.)

The funerals of many of the great names of British history have taken place at Golders Green over the last century, including people from the worlds of politics, films, theatre, music and the arts. They include Neville Chamberlain, Peter Sellers, Ronnie Scott, Lionel Bart, Larry Adler, Ivor Novello, Bram Stoker, Ray Ellington, T. S. Elliot, Edwin Lutyens, Vivien Leigh, Stanley Baldwin, Henry James, Joyce Grenfell, Irene Handl, Keith Moon, Rudyard Kipling, Bud Flanagan, Enid Blyton, Ernest Bevin, Sid James, Marc Bolan, Kingsley Amis, H. G. Wells, Joe Orton, Anna Pavlova, Sigmund Freud, Amy Winehouse and many more. There are also grave locations for 14 holders of the Victoria Cross. A map of the Gardens of Remembrance and information about those cremated here are available from the office.

> The gardens contain many beautiful statues and mausoleums, including the Lutyens-designed Philipson Family mausoleum and the Martin Smith mausoleum (Paul Phipps), which are listed monuments.

The 12 acres (4.9ha) of gardens are extensively planted and provide a beautiful and tranquil environment for visitors. There are several large tombs, two ponds and other water features, a bridge, a large crocus lawn and a special children's section, which includes a swinging bench. There's even a 'communist corner', which includes notables of the Communist Party of Great Britain and the first Soviet ambassador to Britain, Leonid Krasin. There are also two cremation chapels and a chapel of remembrance.

Address: Kilburn Park Road, NW6 5XB (020-7624 1637, saugustinekilburn.
org.uk)

Opening hours: There are no special visiting times, but the church is
open around half an hour before and after services (see website) and Sat
9am-3pm.

Cost: free

Transport: Kilburn Park tube

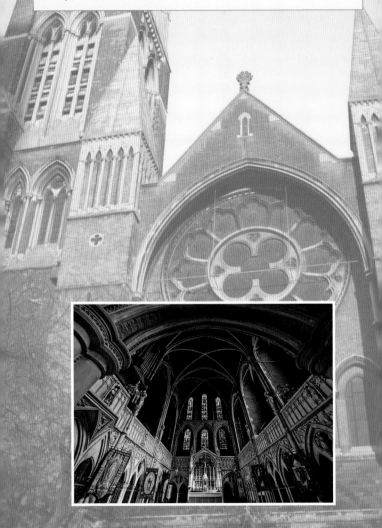

ST AUGUSTINE'S, KILBURN

Saint Augustine's is a magnificent Victorian Gothic Revival church (Grade I listed) which, thanks to its large scale and ornate architecture, is affectionately referred to as the 'Cathedral of North London'. With its soaring vaults and elaborate decoration, it's the ultimate architectural expression of the Catholic Revival of the Church of England which, in the words of its architect, John Loughborough Pearson (1817-1897), truly 'draws people to their knees'.

The church has its roots in the Oxford or Tractarian Movement, a tradition which is now well-established in the Church of England and usually referred to as Anglo-Catholicism (a challenge to Roman Catholicism). St Augustine's was one of a large number of Victorian churches built to witness Tractarian or Anglo-Catholic ideals.

Pearson's plans called for a red brick structure, vaulted ceilings, and extensive interior stone sculpture, reminiscent of 13th-century Gothic architecture. The church (commissioned by Father Kirkpatrick in 1871) was consecrated in 1880, but the tower and spire, remarkable for such Victorian era structures, weren't constructed until 1897-1898. Externally, the design is a balance of soaring steeple (254 feet/77m) and high nave (28 feet/9m wide) with ten bays and a crossing bounded by transepts on the north and south sides.

St Augustine's abounds in glorious religious art which depicts popular biblical stories. Clayton and Bell created the stained glass windows, which include a large rose window depicting the creation, nine clerestory windows (five with angels), nave windows portraying English Saints, a window showing Saint Augustine and several tall lancet windows. Paintings around the nave portray the healing ministry of Jesus of Nazareth. The chancel and sanctuary are enclosed on all four sides by densely carved stone arcades that depict the passion, crucifixion, burial and resurrection of Christ, as well as the apostles, saints and other religious iconography.

> Sir Giles Gilbert Scott (1880-1960) – the designer of the iconic red telephone box – designed the reredos (altar screens) for the high altar in 1930, and also the reredos of the Lady Chapel and the Stations of the Cross.

The south transept leads to the exquisite Chapel of St Michael, with colourful depictions of the Eucharist, sacrifice, angels and the worship of heaven. The Lady Chapel contains frescoes of the Christ child and a later carving of Jesus' presentation in the temple. To complete the Anglo-Catholic tradition, there's a rich collection of embroidery on banners, altar frontals and vestments.

Address: **Alexandra Palace Way, N22 7AY (20-8365 2121, alexandrapalace. com)**

Opening hours: **unrestricted access**

Cost: **free**

Transport: **Wood Green tube**

ALEXANDRA PALACE & PARK

Alexandra Palace (Grade II listed) – named after the Princess of Wales, Alexandra of Denmark (wife of Edward VII) – opened in 1873 to provide Victorians with a recreation centre within a green environment, but was destroyed by fire just 16 days later. A new Palace opened less than two years later, on 1st May 1875, covering an area of some 7.5 acres (3ha), situated in the beautiful Alexandra Park (196 acres/79ha).

The Palace – dubbed the 'People's Palace' – was built by the Lucas Brothers, who also built the Royal Albert Hall at around the same time, and was centred on the Great Hall, home to the mighty Willis Organ driven by two steam engines and vast bellows. The Palace contained a concert hall, art galleries, museum, lecture hall, library, banqueting room and a theatre. There was also an open-air swimming pool (now long closed) and a racecourse with a grandstand (which closed in 1970), a Japanese village, a switchback ride, a boating lake, and a nine-hole pitch & putt golf course.

In 1935 the east wing of the Palace – affectionately nicknamed 'Ally Pally' by Gracie Fields – became the headquarters of the BBC, which made the world's first public television transmissions from here in 1936. It was the main transmitting centre for the BBC until 1956 and its iconic radio tower is still in use today. The original Studios still survive in the southeast wing with their producers' galleries, and are used to exhibit historical television equipment. The original Victorian theatre with its stage machinery also survives.

Just six months after the transfer of trusteeship to Haringey Council, on 10th July 1980, the Palace caught fire for the second time, destroying the Great Hall and Banqueting Suite, the former roller rink and the theatre dressing rooms. Only Palm Court and the area occupied by the BBC escaped damage. It has since been restored and is used nowadays mostly as an exhibition centre, music venue and conference centre.

The grounds boast a pub and restaurant, two cafés, a huge ice rink, boating lake, pitch & putt course, children's play area, deer enclosure, conservation area and 1,500 free parking spaces.

Ally Pally has been a centre of music, sport and events for almost 150 years and remains a popular recreation area, with a wealth of facilities and miles of picturesque walks affording panoramic views of London.

Address: Lordship Lane, N17 8NU (020-8808 8772, haringey.gov.uk/brucecastlemuseum)

Opening hours: castle Wed-Sun 1-5pm, park unrestricted access

Cost: free

Transport: Seven Sisters or Wood Green tube

BRUCE CASTLE, PARK & MUSEUM

Bruce Castle (Grade I listed) is a 16th-century manor house set in 20 acres (8ha) of parkland. The building is constructed of red brick and has been substantially remodelled over the years, notably in the 16th and 17th centuries. Its principal façade has ashlar quoining and tall paned windows and is terminated by symmetrical matching bays. The house and its detached tower are among the earliest examples of a brick building in England.

For the origin of the house's name, we need to go back over 900 years. At the time of the Norman Conquest the manor of Tottenham belonged to Waltheof, Earl of Huntingdon, who married the Conqueror's niece, Judith. Their daughter, Maud, married David I, King of Scotland, who acquired the Earldom of Huntingdon (Waltheof having been executed for treason in 1075). Eventually, the manor passed to the Bruis (or Bruce) family of Scotland, who built the original manor house in 1254. The family's English lands were seized by Edward I in 1306, after Robert the Bruce became King of Scotland. However, the house wasn't renamed Bruce Castle until the 17th century – having previously been called 'Lordship House' – by Henry Hare, 2nd Baron (later Lord) Coleraine (1636-1708), who wanted a grander name (one of his wives is said to haunt the building).

The family of Sir Rowland Hill (1795-1879) – who reformed the British postal system and introduced the Penny Post – ran a progressive boys' school at Bruce Castle from 1827

Sir William Compton (1482-1528), a member of Henry VIII's court, acquired an existing house on the site in 1514 and comprehensively rebuilt it, parts of which are believed to remain today. In 1516, Henry VIII met his sister Margaret, Queen of Scots, here and Elizabeth I was a guest of Sir William's grandson Henry in 1593.

to 1891. The building and the land were purchased in 1891 by Tottenham Urban District Council, and Bruce Castle opened as a museum in 1906 housing local history collections, along with an exhibition about postal history.

Bruce Castle Park became the first public park in Tottenham in 1892, where a famous landmark is a 400-year-old oak tree, a rare survivor of the ancient forest that once covered the area. The park contains a formal rose garden and a Holocaust memorial garden, and also has a playground with paddling pool and tennis and basketball courts. During the year it hosts a variety of festivals and events, including the Tottenham Community Festival and Carnival in June.

Address: Lloyd Park, Forest Road, E17 4PP (020-8496 4390, wmgallery.org.uk, friendsofthewmg.org.uk)

Opening hours: Tue-Sun 10am-5pm

Cost: free

Transport: Walthamstow Central tube

William Morris

WILLIAM MORRIS GALLERY

The William Morris Gallery is delightfully housed in a substantial (Grade II* listed) Georgian dwelling – the Morris' family home from 1848 to 1856 – set in Lloyd Park in Walthamstow. Morris, who was born in Walthamstow, lived here with his widowed mother and his eight brothers and sisters, from the age of 14 to 22. The Gallery is the only public gallery devoted to William Morris (1834-1896) – artist, designer, writer, socialist, conservationist, and father of the Arts and Crafts Movement – and is home to an internationally important collection illustrating his life, achievements and influence.

The house is a superb example of Georgian domestic architecture dating from around 1744. Records indicate that there was a house on the site – or perhaps on the moated 'island' to the rear of the present house – as far back as the 15th century. The existing house was variously known as The Winns or Water House, the latter deriving from the ornamental moat at the back of the house.

A map of 1758 shows the building with its original east and west wings, but without the two semi-circular bays on the south front which were added some thirty or forty years later. Today only the west wing of the original building remains, the east wing having been demolished in the early 1900s. (A recent development created an extension on the site of the former east wing, restoring the symmetry of the building.) One of the finest exterior features is the Corinthian-style porch, its fluted columns and elaborately carved capitals executed in timber, with rosettes used as decorative motifs on the canopy soffit.

> The house and grounds were purchased in 1856 by the publisher Edward Lloyd (1815-1890), whose family donated them to the people of Walthamstow; Lloyd Park – renamed in Edward Lloyd's memory – opened in July 1900.

The William Morris Gallery was opened in 1950 by Prime Minister Clement Attlee and illustrates Morris' life, work and influence. It includes printed, woven and embroidered fabrics, rugs, carpets, wallpapers, furniture, stained glass and painted tiles, designed by Morris and others who together established the firm of Morris, Marshall, Faulkner & Company in 1861.

The Gallery reopened in 2012 after a major redevelopment – at a cost of over £5 million – with innovative new displays, a new tea room, a dedicated learning and research centre, and an exciting programme of temporary exhibitions, activities and events for all ages.

Address: Greenway Close, N4 2EY (020-8356 3000, hackney.gov.uk/
clissold-park and clissoldpark.com)

Opening hours: 7.30am-dusk, café 8.30am-4pm

Cost: free

Transport: Arsenal or Finsbury Park tube

CLISSOLD PARK & HOUSE

Clissold Park is a much-loved public park in Stoke Newington (Hackney), covering 55 acres (22ha), while Clissold House (Grade II* listed) was reputedly designed by Joseph Woods (1776-1864) for his uncle, the Quaker banker Jonathan Hoare (1752-1819). (Had Woods designed the house, which it's thought was built in 1790, he would have been aged around 14!) Financial difficulties forced Hoare to sell the house in 1811 to the Crawshay iron-making family; Eliza Crawshay inherited the property on her father's death in 1835, when she married the Reverend Augustus Clissold (1797-1882), from whom the house and park get their name. On Clissold's death, the estate was bought by developers, but activists John Runtz and Joseph Beck convinced the authorities to buy it and create a public park, which opened in 1889.

Clissold House is a rather severe building with two storeys at the front and three at the rear. An impressive double carriageway leads to a flight of steps and a cut stone porch running the full width of the house, while six-reeded stone Doric columns support a plain, stone balcony, with stone pillars and cast iron railings on three sides. The house was carefully sited to take full advantage of the New River (infilled during the '50s), which carved its way through the park.

Around ten years ago Hackney Council (the current owner) and the Heritage Lottery Fund invested some £10 million in restoring the house and park

> Clissold Park offers a wide range of facilities, including a children's playground, paddling pool, sports fields, bowling green, table tennis, basketball and tennis courts, bandstand, a café and animal attractions, including an aviary, deer paddock and terrapins in the lakes. It's also home to a rich variety of trees and shrubs, a rose garden and an organic nature garden.

to their former glory, which was completed at the end of 2011. The project reinstated original design features to the house and included a new café with improved access for the disabled, restored function rooms, and smaller meeting rooms for private hire and community use. The park has been landscaped, ponds and part of the New River restored, and the facilities improved, including a larger playground and landscaped play area, a wheels park, and a games area for five-a-side football and basketball. The result is one of London's most beautiful and well-equipped parks – even the delightful benches are special in Clissold Park.

1. Pitzhanger Manor & Walpole Park
2. Gunnersbury Park & Museum
3. London Museum of Water & Steam
4. William Hogarth's House
5. Syon House & Park
6. York House Gardens
7. Orleans House Gallery
8. Wimbledon Windmill & Museum
9. Buddhapadipa Temple
10. St Mary's Church
11. Cannizaro Park
12. Southside House
13. Morden Hall Park

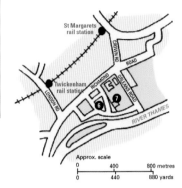

Approx. scale

| 0 | 400 | 800 metres |
| 0 | 440 | 880 yards |

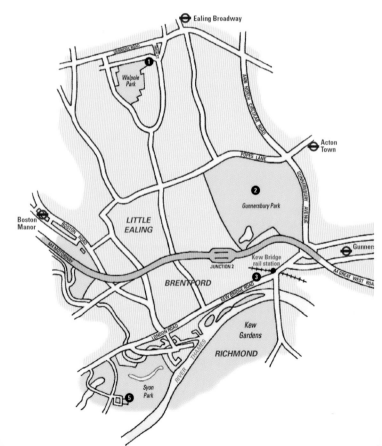

CHAPTER 7

WEST & SOUTHWEST LONDON

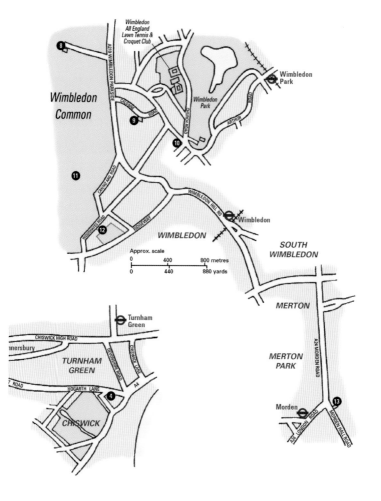

AT A GLANCE

Address: Mattock Lane, W5 5EQ (020-3994 0962, pitzhanger.org.uk and pitzhanger.org.uk/about/walpole-park)

Opening hours: park 7.30am-dusk, house Tue-Fri 10am-4.30pm, Sat 10am-3pm, Sun 10am-4.30pm, closed Mon

Cost: free

Transport: Ealing Broadway tube

PITZHANGER MANOR & WALPOLE PARK

Pitzhanger Manor (PM) is Ealing's flagship cultural venue, comprising the Grade I listed house and the PM Gallery, west London's premier contemporary arts venue. A large house has stood on the site since at least the late 17th century, at which time a smaller Pitzhanger Manor (previously spelled 'Pitshanger') stood a mile or so to its north.

In 1800, the architect Sir John Soane (1753-1837) – designer of the Bank of England and the Dulwich Picture Gallery – purchased the house and around 28 acres (11ha), now Walpole Park, to build a country residence. He demolished most of the existing manor, apart from an extension designed in 1768 by his first employer, George Dance (1741-1825), and created his own home which he used as a showcase for his idiosyncratic architectural style, with its stripped classical detail, radical colour schemes, and inventive use of space and light.

In 1810, Soane sold the house, which had a succession of owners until 1843, when it passed into the Walpole family and became home to the four unmarried daughters of Britain's only assassinated Prime Minister, Spencer Perceval (1762-1812). In 1899, Perceval's grandson, Sir Spencer Walpole (1839-1907) – after whom the park is now named – sold it to Ealing District Council.

> The grounds were opened as a public park in 1901, while the house was extended and became Ealing's public library. In 1984, the library was moved and restoration of the house was begun to reveal its original splendour. The 1939 extension became the Pitzhanger Manor (PM) Gallery in 1996.

Walpole Park (Grade II listed) contains an ornamental bridge (Grade II* listed) remodelled by Soane, a pond (on whose banks he allegedly sat and fished with his friend J.M.W. Turner, the painter), a rose garden and a community kitchen garden. The borough surveyor, Charles Jones (1830-1913), designed the tree-lined avenues, paths and flower beds in the wider park, and planted the sides of the pond nearest the house (originally much deeper) with plants and shrubs. Walpole Park, being a formal park consisting largely of mown grass and large trees, isn't a major attraction to wildlife, although it's edged with diverse plants that provide a habitat for a variety of birds and mammals. The cedar trees on the west lawn date back to the 18th century.

In 2013, the park's historic features and landscapes were restored to reflect Soane's time, which was followed by a (Heritage Lottery Funded) major three-year conservation project to return Pitzhanger Manor to Soane's original design, which reopened in March 2019.

GUNNERSBURY PARK & MUSEUM

Gunnersbury Park in Brentford covers 186 acres (75ha) and contains two early 19th-century mansions, one of which (the Large Mansion) is Grade II* listed and home to Gunnersbury Park Museum. The name *Gunnersbury* derives from Gunylda, the niece of King Canute who lived here until her banishment from England in 1044. The manor, owned by the Bishop of London, was occupied by Sir Thomas Frowyk in the 15th century and in the mid-17th century was acquired by Sir John Maynard, a lawyer and politician, during the time of Cromwell. He built Gunnersbury House, a Palladian mansion designed by John Webb (1611-1672), a pupil and son-in-law of Inigo Jones (1573-1652).

In 1760, the house and estate were purchased for Princess Amelia, favourite daughter of George II, as a country summer retreat, and she landscaped the park in the 18th-century style. After Amelia died in 1786, the estate had a number of owners until

> The museum occupies a suite of grand reception rooms designed by Sydney Smirke (1797-1877) in 1835-6, and has a servants' wing with magnificent original Victorian kitchens (open to the public at weekends from April to October).

John Morley demolished the mansion in 1801 and divided up the estate. Alexander Copland was one of two separate buyers who built the two ('large' and 'small') mansions. In 1835, the merchant and financier Nathan Mayer Rothschild (1777-1836) purchased the 'Large Mansion' and in 1889 the 'Small Mansion' and its grounds were also acquired by the Rothschilds, thus reuniting the original estate. The Rothschilds extended Gunnersbury further, acquiring most of Old Brentford Common Field to the west, as well as land to the north.

The estate was sold to Ealing & Acton Councils in 1925 and the house was opened to the public by Neville Chamberlain, then Minister of Health, in 1926. Since 1929, it has been the home of Gunnersbury Park Museum, the local history museum for the London boroughs of Ealing and Hounslow. The museum contains a wide range of objects, paintings and photographs reflecting life in Ealing and Hounslow, from prehistory to the present day. A multimillion-pound, four-year restoration of the large mansion was completed in June 2018.

Gunnersbury Park contains many exceptional mature trees, open grassland, formal gardens, lakes and historic buildings, including an orangery, Princess Amelia's 18th-century bathhouse, Gothic ruins and stables. The park's facilities include a café, bowling green, an 18-hole pitch and putt golf course, two large play areas (with football, rugby and cricket pitches) and 15 tennis courts.

AT A GLANCE

Address: Green Dragon Lane, TW8 0EN (020-8568 4757, waterandsteam.org.uk)

Opening hours: Wed-Sun 10am-4pm, closed Mon-Tue

Cost: adults £11.25, concessions £9.90, children (5-15) £4.95.

Transport: Kew Bridge rail or Gunnersbury tube

LONDON MUSEUM OF WATER & STEAM

The London Museum of Water & Steam – formerly the Kew Bridge Steam Museum – is a unique museum of water supply, housing a magnificent collection of steam engines and diesel-powered water pumping machines. Although this may not immediately set the pulse racing, it's a fascinating museum that allows visitors to see how London's water supply evolved over the last 2,000 years, from Roman times to the present day.

It's housed within Georgian and Italianate buildings in the Kew Bridge Pumping Station, opened in 1838 by the Grand Junction Waterworks Company. The station supplied west Londoners with water for over 100 years and closed in 1944. The Metropolitan Water Board decided not to scrap the resident steam pumping engines and set them aside to form the basis of a museum display, which eventually opened in 1975, two years after the formation of the Kew Bridge Engines Trust. Today Kew is an internationally-recognised museum of steam pumping engines and the most important historic site of the water supply industry in Britain.

The museum houses the world's largest collection of Cornish beam engines (developed in Cornwall but the name also refers to the engine's operating cycle), including the largest working

> The London Museum of Water & Steam is an absorbing trip back in time to a gentler, slower age, when steam was king and British engineering spanned the globe.

beam engine, the spectacular Grand Junction 90 Engine, used to pump water for 98 years. It has a cylinder diameter of 90 inches, is over 40ft (12m) high and weighs some 250 tons. In 2008, the museum completed the restoration of its Bull Engine (built in 1856), one of only four known examples in the world and the only engine in its original location and still operating. The steam pumping engines are run each weekend and on bank holiday Mondays, the rotative engines operate for three weeks each month, while the Cornish steam engines are run once a month during 'Giants of Steam' weekends (see website).

The steam museum is also home to London's only operating steam railway. The 2ft (610mm) narrow gauge railway is operated by volunteers and in 2009 saw the debut of the museum's new Wren class locomotive, 'Thomas Wicksteed', following the departure of the previous 'Cloister' engine. The line runs for 400 yards (366m) around the Kew Bridge site, with passenger trains operating on Sundays during the summer, bank holiday Mondays and 'special' days. The museum has a café, garden (where you can have a picnic) and a car park for 50 cars.

William Hogarth

WILLIAM HOGARTH'S HOUSE

Hogarth's House (Grade I listed) is the former country home of the famous 18th-century English painter, engraver and satirist William Hogarth (1697-1764), where he lived (with his wife, wife's cousin, mother-in-law and sister) from 1749 until his death in 1764. It provided a quiet summer retreat from the bustle of city life around Hogarth's main house and studio, in what is now Leicester Square.

The house was built between 1713 and 1717 in the corner of an orchard belonging to the Downes family. Its first occupant was the Rev George Andreas Ruperti, the Lutheran pastor of St Mary-le-Savoy in the Strand. Hogarth purchased it from his son in 1749 and extended it in 1750, and his widow added a single-storey extension in 1769.

Hogarth was born near Smithfield Market in London, where his childhood was blighted by his father's imprisonment for

> After visiting the house, take a few minutes to visit Hogarth's tomb in the graveyard of nearby St Nicholas' church.

debt. He was apprenticed to a silver engraver, which gave him skills that helped him produce prints and teach himself to paint. Hogarth hated injustice, snobbery and pretension, and deplored the degradation suffered by the poor. One of his best-known images, *Gin Lane*, has come to represent the worst aspects of slum life in 18th-century London. Hogarth was a shrewd businessman and sold his prints at relatively modest prices, thus reaching a much wider audience than the few who could afford his paintings.

Hogarth's House was opened to the public in 1904 by a local landowner and Hogarth enthusiast, Lieutenant-Colonel Robert William Shipway (1841-1925), who gave the house to Middlesex County Council in 1907. The house was damaged in 1941 during World War Two but was repaired and reopened in 1951. It was restored again for the Hogarth Tercentenary in 1997 and closed again for refurbishment in September 2008, during which it was badly damaged by fire in 2009, which led to the house remaining closed until November 2011.

Two floors of the house are now open to the public and contain the most extensive collection of Hogarth's prints on permanent public display. The panelled rooms also house some replica pieces of 18th-century furniture. An exhibition documents Hogarth's life and work with copies of his best-known series of engravings, including *A Harlot's Progress*, *A Rake's Progress* and *Marriage à-la-mode*. The house has an attractive walled garden containing fruit trees and a mulberry tree that's at least 300 years old.

Address: Syon Park, Brentford, TW8 8JF (020-8560 0882, syonpark.co.uk)

Opening hours: house, Mar-Oct 11am-5pm on selected days (see website), gardens 10.30am-5pm

Cost: House, gardens and Great Conservatory £13, concessions £11.50, children (5-16) £6, family (2 adults, 2 children) £30. Gardens and Great Conservatory £8, concessions £6.50, children £4.50, family £18.

Transport: Gunnersbury or Ealing Broadway tube then **237 or 267 bus to Brent Lea bus stop or E2 or E8 bus to Brentford**

SYON HOUSE & PARK

Although situated in less-than-glamorous Brentford, Syon House and its 200-acre (80ha) park (both Grade I listed) comprise one of England's finest estates with a rich history. The name derives from Syon Abbey, a medieval monastery of the Bridgettine Order founded in 1415 by Henry V. It moved to the site now occupied by Syon House in 1431 and was dissolved in 1539 during the Dissolution of the Monasteries.

In 1594, Henry Percy, 9th Earl of Northumberland, acquired Syon House through his marriage to Dorothy Devereux, and the Percy family have lived there ever since. In 1750, Sir Hugh Smithson inherited the Percy estates through his wife, Elizabeth Seymour, and they revived the Percy name, when Sir Hugh became Earl and later 1st Duke of Northumberland in 1766. In 1761 he commissioned architect and interior designer Robert Adam (1728-1792) and landscape designer Lancelot 'Capability' Brown (1716-1783) to redesign the house and estate. While Adam's architecture was inspired by classical Rome, Brown took the medieval deer park as his model.

Adam's plans for the interior of Syon House included a complete suite of rooms on the principal level, together with a rotunda in the main courtyard (not built). In the event, only five main rooms were completed (in the Neo-classical style) on the west, south and east sides of the House, from the Great Hall to the Long Gallery. But Syon House is feted as Adam's early English masterpiece and is the finest surviving evidence of his revolutionary use of colour. Two rooms sum up Adam's genius: the grand scale and splendour of the Great Hall, which resembles the Imperial Rome of a Hollywood epic, and – in dramatic contrast, the richly-decorated Ante Room or Vestibule, with its riot of coloured marble – one of Adam's most ingenious and original designs.

> Syon House remains the London home of the Duke of Northumberland and is the last surviving ducal residence complete with its country estate in Greater London.

Within the 200 acres (81ha) of parkland there are 40 acres (16ha) of gardens and an ornamental lake, renowned for their extensive collection of over 200 species of rare trees. The crowning glory of the gardens is the Great Conservatory, designed by Charles Fowler (1792-1867) and completed in 1830, which was the first large-scale conservatory built from metal and glass. However, although the park and lake were designed by Capability Brown in 1760, today they have a 19th-century character.

Address: Richmond Road, Twickenham, TW1 3AA (08456-122 660, richmond.gov.uk > York House Gardens and yorkhousesociety.org.uk)

Opening hours: dawn-dusk

Cost: free

Transport: Twickenham rail

YORK HOUSE GARDENS

York House (Grade II listed) is a fine 17th-century building with a fascinating history, set in beautiful grounds on the banks of the River Thames. The riverside gardens were commissioned by Sir Ratan Tata (1871-1918), a Parsee from Mumbai who purchased the house from the Duc d'Orleans in 1906 (after whom Orleans House is named – see next entry). Tata, whose family still runs one of the largest industrial companies in India, installed striking statues of naked female figures in the gardens.

The statues represent the Oceanides or sea nymphs of Greek mythology, and include two winged horses with a female charioteer in a shell chariot, plunging through the water at the top of a cascade and pool, while seven other figures are posed sitting on rocks or clambering up them.

The statues were brought to England to adorn Lea Park (now Witley Park) near Godalming, Surrey, by the financier Whitaker Wright, but were sold in 1904 after he was found guilty of fraud and committed suicide. The fin-de-siècle sculptures (Grade II listed) are carved in Italian white Carrera marble by an unknown sculptor, although it's thought they came from the Roman studio of Orazio Andreoni at the turn of the 19th century. After decades of neglect the statues were restored in 1988 thanks to Elizabeth Bell-Wright, who encouraged the York House Society and the Twickenham Society to save them.

York House Gardens comprise a diverse range of areas, including tennis courts, formal planting, amenity grass and woodland. Around the recently restored cascades, planting has been designed

> Some of the statues are in highly unusual attitudes and can come as a great surprise to the unsuspecting visitor.

to harmonise with the statues, with greens, pinks and whites predominating. The aquatic planting in the pool has also been improved with additional water lilies, irises and arum lilies, while candelabra primulas were planted extensively around the water's edge. Some unusual specimen trees and shrubs have also been added to enliven the landscaping, including several types of magnolia, *cornus controversa* and tulip trees, and there's a beautifully restored Japanese garden, too.

Although the house isn't officially open to the public – being the HQ of the London borough of Richmond (which purchased it in 1924 to use as offices) – it's a public building and parts of it are open on occasions (it can also be rented for weddings and other events).

AT A GLANCE

Address: **Riverside, Twickenham, TW1 3DJ (020-8831 6000, orleanshousegallery.org)**

Opening hours: **Tue-Sun 10am-5pm, closed Mon**

Cost: **free**

Transport: **Twickenham rail**

Louis Phillipe I, Duc d'Orleans

ORLEANS HOUSE GALLERY

The Orleans House Gallery is one of Greater London's finest small galleries, located in woodland overlooking the Thames. It opened in 1972 and is home to the London borough of Richmond-upon-Thames' art collection, one of the most outstanding fine art collections in London outside the city's national collections, comprising some 3,200 paintings, drawings, photographs, prints and objects dating from the early 18th century to the present day. The collection contains oil paintings, watercolours, drawings and prints by notable artists, including: Peter Tillemans (1684-1734), Samuel Scott (c1702-1772), Jean-Baptiste-Camille Corot (1796-1875) and Eric Fraser (1902-1983).

The original Thames-side house was built in 1710 for James Johnston (1655-1737), Joint Secretary of State for Scotland under William III, by John James (1672-1746). In stark contrast to the rather plain house, the ornate baroque Octagon Room – designed by the renowned architect James Gibbs (1682-1754) – was built as a garden pavilion in around 1720 for lavish entertainment (Queen Caroline, the wife of George II, dined there in 1729).

Orleans House has a rich and vibrant history and takes its name from its most famous resident, Louis Philippe I, Duc d'Orleans (1773-1850), who lived here from 1815 to 1817 during his exile from Napoleonic France (and who was the king of France from 1830 to 1847). Most of the house was demolished in 1926 but the Octagon and two wings were saved by the Hon. Mrs Nellie Ionides (1883-1962), who bequeathed the riverside property and 500 portraits to Richmond borough to create a public gallery.

The gallery has a reputation for its innovative exhibitions and hosts a number of exhibitions a year in the main gallery, ranging from historical exhibitions of works from the permanent collection to contemporary exhibitions of painting, photographs, crafts and ceramics. Each exhibition features a changing themed display of works ('In Focus') from the permanent collection. The nearby Stables Gallery (opened in 1994) is housed in the evocative 19th-century stable buildings, and exhibits work by up-and-coming, avant-garde artists, local artists, and community groups and organisations.

> The simple exterior belies the stunning baroque interior, decorated by the renowned Swiss stuccatori Guiseppe Artari and Giovanni Bagutti, who also decorated St Martin-in-the-Fields church in central London.

In addition to the two galleries and the Octagon Room (available for hire), there's the Coach House Education Centre, an artist in residence studio, a shop and the Stables Café (Tue-Sun 9am-5pm). See website for information about exhibitions, activities and festivals.

AT A GLANCE

Address: Windmill Road, Wimbledon, SW19 5NR (020-8947 2825, wimbledonwindmill.org.uk)

Opening hours: End of March to October Sat 2-5pm, Sun and bank holiday Mon 10am-5pm

Cost: free

Transport: Wimbledon train/tube then 93 bus to Windmill Road

WIMBLEDON WINDMILL & MUSEUM

The Wimbledon Windmill Museum is – reassuringly and appropriately – housed in a windmill in the middle of Wimbledon Common, and offers an enjoyable day out for families. The Common is just 8 miles (5km) from central London, yet comprises 1,140 acres (461ha) of natural open space beloved by walkers, runners, cyclists, horse riders, golfers and nature lovers (et al).

Wimbledon Windmill was built by Charles March in 1817 and operated until 1864, when the miller was evicted by the 5th Earl Spencer, who wanted to enclose the land and build himself a grand manor house. The locals opposed him and in 1871 an Act of Parliament was passed giving the people right of access to the Commons in perpetuity. By this time the mill machinery had been removed, so the mill was converted into residential accommodation (one room has been preserved as it was when the mill accommodated no fewer than six families).

In 1976 the building became a museum and the sails were later restored to working order (they're occasionally run when there's sufficient wind). The design of the windmill is unusual, with a two-storey octagonal base, originally of brick and timber, where the working machinery was housed, and a conical tower supporting the cap where the sails are mounted. It was built as a hollow post mill, with the drive to the stones passing through the centre of the main post, but was rebuilt as a smock mill when it was preserved in 1893.

The museum's displays are on two levels. The ground floor exhibits relate mainly to the development

The museum also contains a display of Scouting memorabilia – Robert Baden-Powell (1857-1941), founder of the Boy Scouts, partially wrote *Scouting for Boys* in the Mill House in 1908.

and construction of windmills, and include a model room with operating models of different types of windmill, tracing the development of windmills from early Greek and Persian mills to modern wind farms, including some unusual and experimental mills. A video room shows a continuous film on the design, construction and operation of English windmills, and there's also an extensive collection of millwright's tools. Upstairs, exhibits explain in detail how the windmill worked and how grain was milled to produce flour. Children can try their hand at milling flour using a saddle stone, a mortar and a hand quern.

A small shop sells souvenirs, books, postcards and even Wombles – who, of course, live on Wimbledon Common – and there's an independent café next door.

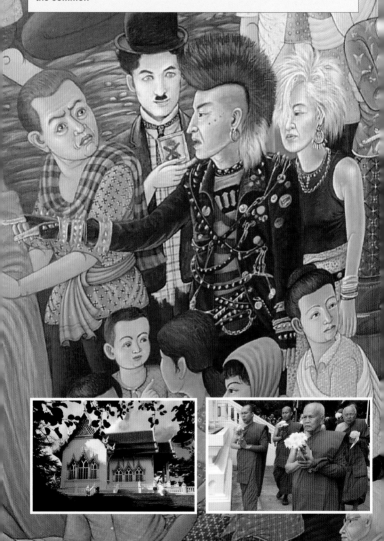

Address: 14 Calonne Road, Wimbledon Parkside, SW19 5HJ (020-8946 1357, watbuddhapadipa.org)

Opening hours: grounds 9.30am-5/6pm. The main temple is open at weekends or by appointment.

Cost: free

Transport: Wimbledon rail/tube then 93 bus towards Putney and alight at the common

BUDDHAPADIPA TEMPLE

This is Europe's only purpose-built Thai temple, established by the London Buddhist Temple Foundation to create a centre for the dissemination of theoretical and practical Buddhist teachings, which has become one of Europe's most important Buddhist training centres. Its full name is Wat Buddhapadipa, a Wat being a Buddhist sacred precinct with monks' quarters, the temple proper, an edifice housing a large image of Buddha and a structure for lessons.

The grounds of the Wat cover approximately 4 acres (1.6ha) in which the Uposatha Hall (temple) is situated on an ornamental lake, with a small grove, flower garden and an orchard. The temple consists of the house where the monks live and a cottage. On the ground floor of the house there's a shrine room, dining room, study, library, cloakroom, office, kitchen and telephone room. The rest of the House is private accommodation for the monks.

The Uposatha Hall is a beautiful building with traditional white walls contrasted by the red and gold of the roof, windows and doors. It was designed in accordance with Thai architectural principles and is composed of four-gabled roofs known as Caturamuk. The inauguration ceremony was performed by HRH Princess Kallayanivaddana, the elder sister of the late King of Thailand, on the 30th October 1982.

The Hall contains three Buddha statues: the main one is cast in black bronze and was presented to the temple by the King of Thailand in 1966 (when it was located in Christ Church Road, Richmond). The second (golden) image of the Buddha was presented by the committee of the Foundation Buddhist Temple, while the third

As is traditional, the Ubosot murals contain contemporary figures, including portraits of Mother Teresa and Margaret Thatcher (strange bedfellows), as well as the temple's patrons and the artists themselves.

image is a replica of the Emerald Buddha in the Temple of the Emerald Buddha (known as Wat Phra Keow) at the Grand Palace in Bangkok. The stunning shrine room in the House is dominated by a golden statue of the Buddha – a replica of the Buddhasihing in the National Museum in Bangkok – with various offerings placed before it, while the beautiful murals in the ordination hall or Ubosot depict important episodes from the life of Buddha.

Although the temple is home to monks and nuns, it welcomes visitors of any faith to view the grounds and temple, and offers a wide range of Buddhism and meditation courses.

Address: **30 St Mary's Road, SW19 7BP (020-8946 2605,
stmaryswimbledon.org)**

Opening hours: **Mon-Fri 9am-1pm; see website for service times**

Cost: **free**

Transport: **Wimbledon Park tube**

ST MARY'S CHURCH

St Mary's is a large, Grade II listed, Anglican parish church in Wimbledon. It's built of knapped flint and limestone and replaced an earlier church; in fact it's the fourth church recorded on the site since 1086. The present Victorian building dates from 1843 and was designed by Sir George Gilbert Scott (1811-1878), one of the most famous and prolific Victorian architects.

Scott was given a strict budget of £4,000 for the work, which he managed by incorporating parts of the earlier Georgian building. He extended the old nave westwards and built a new tower and spire (196ft/60m), while the existing Georgian windows were enlarged and given their present perpendicular form, and the weakened walls buttressed at frequent intervals. Scott installed new galleries and a hammer-beam oak roof. Finally, in order to harmonise the old and new, the brickwork was covered with knapped flints.

The painted beams (with a chevron and daisy design) in the chancel are thought to be medieval, while low down on the south side of the chancel is a 'Leper Window', a small barred aperture believed to have been used in medieval times to administer the sacrament to diseased people outside.

The interior has three galleries and a Georgian seating plan with box pews, dating from the 1843 reconstruction. The pulpit dates from 1912, replacing one from 1500, and is now balanced by the Victorian font which was moved to its present position in 1993. There are also a number of notable stained glass windows, including one designed by Henry Holiday and executed by William Morris & Co (another window is also by Morris).

The church has a striking modern Garden Hall (available for hire) built in 2003 – with a glass wall – which has won a number of architectural awards.

The organ was acquired in 1843 and still performs well, having been rebuilt twice. The church bells, whose story is told in a plaque in the west porch, include two that date from the 16th century. The music at Sunday Eucharist (9.30am) and Evensong (6.30pm) is led by St Mary's Church Choir, which tackles everything from Renaissance polyphony and Bach motets to spirituals and Taizé chants.

Along with Chiswick and Hampstead graveyards, St Mary's churchyard possesses the highest concentration of listed monuments anywhere in Greater London, including a number of large monuments such as the mausoleum of Sir Joseph William Bazalgette (1819-1891), the renowned engineer of London's sewer system.

Address: **West Side Common, Wimbledon, SW19 4UE (020-8545 3678, cannizaropark.com and hotelduvin.com/locations/wimbledon)**

Opening hours: **Mon-Fri 8am-dusk, Sat-Sun 9am-dusk**

Cost: **free**

Transport: **Wimbledon tube/rail, then 93 bus to edge of common and 10-minute walk**

CANNIZARO PARK

The lovely Cannizaro Park is a Grade II* listed park of 35 acres (14ha) on the edge of Wimbledon Common, although it sounds as if it should be in Rome. It was a private garden for some 300 years, opened to the public as a park in 1949, and combines great natural beauty with a unique collection of rare and exquisite trees and shrubs, including sassafrass, camellia, rhododendron and other ericaceous plants (it's also noted for its rich wildlife).

It has a large variety of green areas, from expansive lawns to small intimate spaces such as the herb and tennis court gardens, and lovely leisurely walks through the woodlands. Formal areas have been developed, with a sunken garden next to the park's hotel and an Italian Garden near its pond, expressing the changing face of garden design down the years.

Warren House – now Cannizaro House – was built in the early 1700s, when the kitchen garden served the tables of some of its most famous residents and guests, from its 18th-century heyday to the last private owners in the 1940s (the house is now a hotel). The name Cannizaro dates back to 1832 when Count St Antonio leased the house. He later succeeded to the dukedom of Cannizzaro in Sicily and left England to live with his mistress in Milan, but his long-suffering wife, Sophia, prided herself on the title of Duchess of Cannizzaro. When she died in 1841, the estate was recorded under her name, and apart from the spelling change, has stuck ever since.

> The park has a long history of staging arts and musical events (including the Wimbledon Cannizaro Festival in summer), and contains a variety of sculptures, including a statue of Diana and the fawn and an elaborate fountain in the driveway.

With the exception of Viscount Melville (1742-1811), who planted Lady Jane's Wood in 1793, the greatest private contributors to today's park were Mr and Mrs E. Kenneth Wilson who lived there from 1920 to 1947. Their daughter, Hilary, married the 5th Earl of Munster in 1928 and 20 years later (after her parents died) sold the estate to Wimbledon corporation for £40,000.

The park's timeless appeal is a joy at any time – thanks to the tireless efforts of the Friends of Cannizaro Park – and is particularly special in spring when the rhododendrons, azaleas and magnolias are in bloom. Or visit in autumn, when the birch, maple and horse chestnut trees are equally colourful and spectacular.

Address: 3-4 Woodhayes Road, Wimbledon, SW19 4RJ (020-8946 7643, southsidehouse.com)

Opening hours: guided tours (75 mins) from Easter Sun to the last Sun of September on Wed, Sat, Sun and public holidays at 2pm and 3.30pm. The house is closed for Wimbledon tennis fortnight and during the winter.

Cost: adults £9, students £7.50, seniors £5 (Wed 3.30pm), families £20 (2 adults, 2 children under 16)

Transport: Wimbledon tube/rail, then 200 bus to Edge Hill (6-minute walk)

SOUTHSIDE HOUSE

Southside House is a 17th-century property situated (appropriately) on the south side of Wimbledon Common. It was built for Robert Pennington (who shared Charles II's exile in Holland), who commissioned Dutch architects to build the house, incorporating an existing farmhouse into the design. Two niches either side of the front door contain statues of *Plenty* and *Spring*, which are said to bear the likenesses of Pennington's wife and daughter.

Southside was later rebuilt in the William and Mary style; behind the long façade are the old rooms, still with much of the Penningtons' original 17th-century furniture, and a superb collection of art and historical objects reflecting centuries of ownership. The house's 'musik' room was prepared for the entertainment of Frederick, Prince of Wales, who visited in 1750. Later visitors to the house included Sir William and Lady Emma Hamilton, together with Lord Nelson and Lord Byron.

The house passed through the Pennington-Mellor family, eventually coming into the possession of Malcolm Munthe (1910-1995), the son of Hilda Pennington-Mellor (1882-1967) and Axel Munthe (1857-1949), author of *The Story of St Michele*. During World War Two Southside House was damaged and Malcolm Munthe spent much of his later life restoring it. The house survived a fire on 28th November 2010, which caused considerable damage, and after being repaired was officially opened in November 2011.

The gardens are a delightful hotchpotch of wilderness, order, woodland, secret pathways, classical follies and water, which combine to create a garden full of surprises. They're open under the National Gardens

> Described by connoisseurs as an unforgettable experience, Southside House provides an enchantingly eccentric backdrop to the lives and loves of generations of the Pennington-Mellor-Munthe families. Maintained in traditional style without intrusive refurbishment and crammed with centuries of family possessions, it offers a wealth of fascinating family stories.

Scheme during the spring and visitors taking house tours are welcome to wander and explore. Arts and performance events are also staged here.

Today Southside House is still run by Robert Pennington's descendants, serving partly as a residence but also as a museum, administered by the Pennington-Mellor-Munthe Charity Trust. It hosts tour groups – including special **candlelit tours followed by drinks and a buffet supper –** and cultural events such as lectures, concerts and literary discussions.

Address: **Morden Hall Road, SM4 5JD (020-8545 6850, nationaltrust.org. uk/morden-hall-park)**

Opening hours: **8am-6pm**

Cost: **free**

Transport: **Morden tube**

MORDEN HALL PARK

Morden Hall Park, owned by the National Trust, covers over 125 acres (50ha) of parkland in what was once rural Surrey. This tranquil former deer park is one of the few remaining estates that used to line the River Wandle during its industrial heyday, and contains Morden Hall itself (now an events centre), a stable yard (now restored and containing interactive exhibitions), the pretty Morden Cottage (now a school) situated in the rose garden, and many old farm buildings, some of which house a garden centre and a city farm. Visitors can still see the original waterwheel that (until 1922) turned the massive millstones used to crush tobacco into fine powder. Today the Snuff Mill – one of the original Grade II listed mills – is used as an education centre.

The estate land was originally owned by Westminster Abbey and there's evidence of an earlier manor house, although the current Morden Hall dates from the 1770s. The Hall was home to the Garth family for generations and was a school for young gentlemen in around 1840, until being sold in the 1870s by Sir Richard Garth QC (1820-1903) to a tobacco merchant, Gilliat Hatfeild (1827-1906). Gilliat Hatfeild's son, Gilliat Edward Hatfeild (1864-1941), left the core of the estate (including the Hall) to the National Trust.

Morden Hall Park sits on the flood plain of the beautiful River Wandle and consists of three main habitats: meadowland, marshland and woodland. Water lies at the heart of the park, with the river, mill ponds and a lake. The lush wetlands, riverbanks and islands provide an ideal habitat for a variety of plants, animals, insects and abundant birdlife, including wildfowl, heron and kingfishers. There's an ornamental avenue of lime and horse-chestnut trees, and a mulberry tree thought to have been planted by Huguenots in the 18th century; the park also contains native trees such as oak, beech, ash, birch, and some lovely riverside willows and alders, including one of the oldest yews in England.

> The beautiful rose garden was originally laid out by Gilliat Hatfeild in 1922 and contains some 2,000 roses, including 25 varieties of florabunda roses displayed across 38 flowerbeds. Visit between May and September to enjoy the rich aroma of the roses in full bloom.

The walled kitchen garden once employed 14 gardeners and is now home to the Riverside Café and National Trust shop. There's also a demonstration kitchen garden.

1. Oxo Tower & Gabriel's Wharf
2. Cross Bones Graveyard
3. Borough Market
4. City Hall & Art Gallery
5. Brunel Museum
6. St George the Martyr
7. Florence Nightingale Museum
8. South London Gallery
9. West Norwood Cemetery
10. Crystal Palace Park & Dinosaurs
11. Crossness Pumping Station
12. Hall Place & Gardens
13. Down House (Home of Charles Darwin)
14. Beefeater Gin Distillery

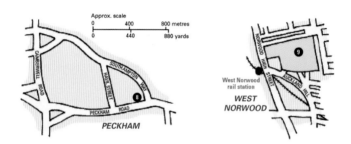

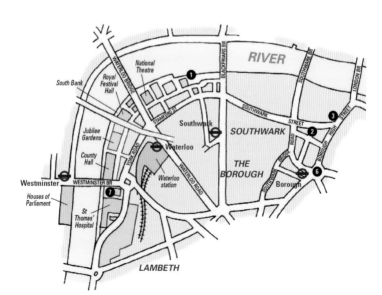

CHAPTER 8

SOUTH & SOUTHEAST LONDON

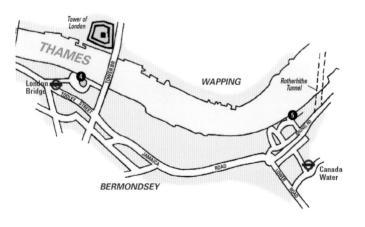

1. Oxo Tower & Gabriel's Wharf
2. Cross Bones Graveyard
3. Borough Market
4. City Hall & Art Gallery
5. Brunel Museum
6. St George the Martyr
7. Florence Nightingale Museum
8. South London Gallery
9. West Norwood Cemetery
10. Crystal Palace Park & Dinosaurs
11. Crossness Pumping Station
12. Hall Place & Gardens
13. Home of Charles Darwin (Down House)
14. Beefeater Gin Distillery

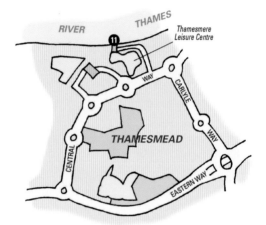

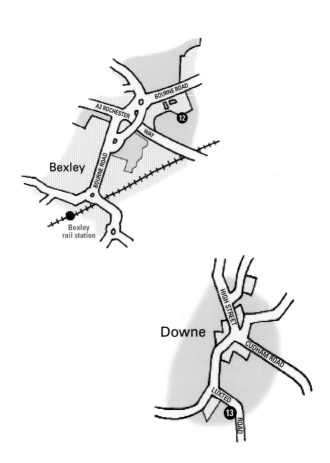

Bexley

A2 ROCHESTER

BOURNE ROAD

WAY

BOURNE ROAD

12

Bexley
rail station

HIGH STREET

Downe

CUDHAM ROAD

LUXTED

ROAD

13

RIVER THAMES

VAUXHALL BRIDGE

KENNINGTON

KENNINGTON LANE

14

Vauxhall

HARLEYFORD RD

PARRY ST

WANDSWORTH ROAD

FENTIMAN ROAD

VAUXHALL

The Oval
Cricket Ground

OXO TOWER & GABRIEL'S WHARF

The OXO Tower Wharf is a building (with a prominent tower) in Southwark on the south bank of the Thames adjacent to Gabriel's Wharf (home to an eclectic mix of independent shops, cafes, bars and restaurants). The tower was constructed at the end of the 19th century as a power station for the Post Office and was subsequently acquired by Liebig's Extract of Meat Company, manufacturers of OXO beef stock cubes, for conversion into a cold store. It was largely rebuilt to an Art Deco design by company architect Albert Moore between 1928 and 1929, when much of the original power station was demolished. Liebig wanted to include a tower featuring illuminated signs advertising the OXO name; when permission was refused the tower was built with four sets of three vertically-aligned windows, each of which was 'coincidentally' in the shapes of a circle, a cross and a circle spelling OXO!

By the '70s the building had fallen into disrepair and was largely derelict, and there were several proposals to demolish and develop it along with the adjacent Coin Street site, which were met with strong local opposition. Permission for redevelopment was eventually granted, but the tower and 13-acre (5.3ha) site were purchased by the Greater London Council in 1984 for £2.7m and sold on to the non-profit Coin Street Community Builders for just £750,000. In the '90s the tower was refurbished to an award-winning design by Lifschutz Davidson as a mixed use development called Oxo Tower Wharf.

On the tower's rooftop is the OXO Tower restaurant, bar and brasserie (operated by Harvey Nichols) and a free public viewing gallery (open daily). The residential area below consists of 78 flats on five floors owned by the Redwood Housing Co-operative. The ground, first and second floors are home to over 30 retail design studios, as well as specialist shops and the gallery@oxo, with a changing programme of exhibitions. A unique feature of Oxo Tower Wharf is its concentration of retail studios for contemporary designers, where you can watch artisans at work and buy a wide variety of original products including fashion, fine art, furniture, textiles, jewellery, ceramics and glass.

> The tower is a splendid sight – particularly at night when the OXO letters are lit up in red – a tribute to its creators, while the wharfs are a shining example of what can be achieved with a derelict site.

OXO Tower Wharf and Gabriel's Wharf are situated on the riverside walkway, part of the Thames Path, a continuous riverside walk that passes in front of and below the OXO Tower, and links to other riverside attractions such as the Festival Hall, the National Theatre, the Tate Modern and the Globe Theatre.

Address: Redcross Way, SE1 1YJ (020-7403 3393, crossbones.org.uk)

Opening hours: No access to the actual burial ground, which is private land, but the gates are accessible and have become a shrine.

Cost: free

Transport: Borough tube

CROSS BONES GRAVEYARD

C ross Bones is a disused, post-medieval burial ground in Southwark. It's believed to have been an unconsecrated graveyard for 'single women' – a euphemism for prostitutes – known locally as 'Winchester Geese', as they were licensed by the Bishop of Winchester to work within the 'Liberty of the Clink' in Southwark.

The age of the graveyard is unknown, but John Stow (1525-1605) wrote about it in *A Survey of London* in 1598, calling it the 'single woman's churchyard'. By 1769 it had become a paupers' graveyard serving the poor of St Saviour's parish, and it's thought that up to 15,000 people were buried here. The graveyard was closed in 1853 because it was 'completely overcharged with dead' and further burials were deemed 'inconsistent with a due regard for the public health and public decency.' The site was sold in 1883 as a building site, which prompted an objection from Lord Brabazon in a letter to *The Times*, asking that the land be saved from 'such desecration'. The sale was declared null and void the following year under the Disused Burial Grounds Act 1884, and subsequent attempts to develop the site were opposed by local people.

Between 1991 and 1998, excavations were conducted by the Museum of London Archaeology Service before the construction of the London underground Jubilee Line. They found a highly overcrowded graveyard with bodies piled on top of each other, most having died from diseases. One dig uncovered around 150 skeletons, almost half of which were perinatal, i.e. between 22 weeks gestation and seven days after birth or less than one year old. The adults were mostly women.

In 1996, local playwright, poet and author John Constable revived the story of Cross Bones and wrote *The Southwark Mysteries*, a cycle of poems and mystery plays inspired by the spirit of

> The 'Clink' lay outside the jurisdiction of the City's walls and became notorious for its brothels and theatres, as well as bull- and bear-baiting – activities that were prohibited within the City itself.

the 'Winchester Geese'. The book, in turn, gave birth to the Cross Bones Halloween Festival, celebrated annually since 1998 with a procession, candles and songs. The Friends of Cross Bones are campaigning for a permanent memorial garden. Meanwhile the iron gates in Redcross Way have been transformed into 'a people's shrine', an inclusive sacred place, with an ever-changing array of messages, ribbons, flowers and other totems, including a bronze plaque bearing the epitaph: 'The Outcast Dead R.I.P.'.

Address: **8 Southwark Street, SE1 1TL (020-7407 1002, boroughmarket. org.uk)**

Opening hours: **Mon-Fri 10am-5pm (6pm Fri), 8am-5pm Sat, closed Sun**

Cost: **free**

Transport: **London Bridge tube/rail**

BOROUGH MARKET

Borough Market is a retail food market in Southwark and the largest food market in London, offering a huge variety of foods sourced from Britain and around the world. The present market is a successor to one that originally adjoined the end of London Bridge. It was first recorded in 1276, although some claim the market has existed since 1014, and probably much earlier. The City of London received a royal charter from Edward VI in 1550 to control all markets in Southwark, which was confirmed by Charles II in 1671. However, the market caused such traffic congestion that in 1754 it was abolished by an Act of Parliament.

The Act did, however, allow the local parishioners to set up another market on a new site, and in 1756 a market was established on a 4.5 acre (1.8ha) site in Rochester Yard (once the churchyard of St Margaret's church). During the 19th century it became one of London's most important food markets thanks to its strategic position near the riverside wharves of the Pool of London. The present buildings were designed in 1851, with additions in the 1860s, with an entrance designed in the Art Deco style added on Southwark Street in 1932. However, this isn't a museum piece but a dynamic, ever-changing institution; a participant in the wider debates around what we eat and where it comes from; a place where food is talked about almost as enthusiastically as it's consumed.

Borough Market, set beneath the railway viaducts between the Thames and Borough High Street, sprawls around an atmospheric warren of streets and walkways; in addition to the labyrinthine central area there are also

> Since its renaissance as a retail market two decades ago, Borough Market has become a mecca for those who care about the quality and provenance of the food they eat, and chefs, restaurateurs, keen amateur cooks, gourmets and gourmands, epicures and foodies all flock here.

two self-contained covered markets – the Jubilee Market and the Green Market. There's a limited market on Mon-Tue, when not all stalls and shops are open and a full market (all shops and stalls open) from Wed-Sat.

The market was historically focused on fruit and vegetables, but in recent decades has added fine food stalls, which includes some of the market's most famous traders such as Artisan du Chocolat, Monmouth Coffee Co, Olivier's Bakery, Furness Fish & Game Supplies and the Spanish company Brindisa. In addition to fresh food, a wide variety of cooked and snack food is available.

CITY HALL & ART GALLERY

City Hall is a striking building in Southwark on the south bank of the Thames. Designed by celebrated architect Norman Foster (b 1935), it cost £65 million and opened in July 2002. Despite the name, City Hall is nothing to do with the City of London (which has its HQ in the Guildhall), but is the headquarters of the Greater London Authority (GLA), which comprises the Mayor of London and the London Assembly. It represents the 32 boroughs of Greater London. (The predecessors of the GLA had their headquarters at County Hall – upstream on the South Bank – now a commercial building.)

City Hall has an unusual bulbous shape, intended to reduce its surface area and improve energy efficiency, and it incorporates many environmentally-friendly features such as solar panels on the roof. It has been variously compared to – among other things – Darth Vader's helmet, a misshapen egg, a fencing mask, a car headlight, a woodlouse and a motorcycle helmet. Former mayor Ken Livingstone referred to it as a 'glass testicle', while mayor Boris Johnson called it (similarly) a 'glass gonad' (he's posh) and, more politely, 'the onion'. Aficionados claim City Hall is one of the most inspired buildings constructed in Europe in years and a bold statement on transparent government, while to its detractors it's a triumph of style over substance (how do you clean the windows?).

A 1,640ft (500m) helical walkway ascends the full height of the ten-storey building, at the top of which is an exhibition and meeting space called 'London's Living Room', with an open viewing deck that's occasionally open to the public. The walkway provides views of the interior of the building and is intended to symbolise transparency.

Don't miss the London Photomat on the floor of the Visitor Centre, which provides an aerial view of the whole of Greater London in precise detail, including recognisable individual houses and buildings.

City Hall has a free art gallery which hosts regular exhibitions, usually on topics relating to London or created by Londoners – there's also a café on the lower ground floor.

Next to City Hall is a sunken amphitheatre (The Scoop), where there's free entertainment in summer, while nearby Potters Fields Park – one of the few remaining open spaces along the riverside – affords great views of the river.

Whether you're keen to view local government in action (there's a 250-seat viewing gallery) or simply wish to enjoy the city skyline, City Hall is well worth a visit.

Address: Railway Avenue, Rotherhithe, SE16 4LF (020-7231 3840, brunel-museum.org.uk)

Opening hours: 10am-5pm

Cost: adults £6, concessions £3, under 16s free

Transport: Rotherhithe rail or Canada Water tube and 10-minute walk

Isambard Kingdom Brunel

Sir Marc Isambard Brunel

BRUNEL MUSEUM

The Brunel Museum celebrates the life and work of three generations of the legendary Brunel engineering family: Sir Marc Isambard Brunel (1769-1849), his more famous son, Isambard Kingdom Brunel (1806-1859) – widely considered to be Britain's greatest ever engineer – and Isambard's second son, Henry Marc Brunel (1842-1903), also a civil engineer.

The museum is situated above the Thames Tunnel in the Brunel Engine House in Rotherhithe – designed by Sir Marc – part of the infrastructure of the Thames Tunnel which contained steam engines to pump water from the tunnel. A permanent exhibition tells the story of the construction and history of the tunnel, including display panels, models of the tunnel under construction, original artefacts and a video presentation.

Marc Isambard Brunel had a fascinating, if turbulent, life. Born in Normandy to a farming family, he became a naval cadet in 1786 and after returning to France during the French Revolution, unwisely predicted the demise of Robespierre and had to flee to New York. He took American citizenship in 1796 and was appointed chief engineer of the city of New York. In 1799 he sailed to England and soon after married Sophia Kingdom (an Englishwoman he had met in France) in 1806.

Among his most notable inventions was the first automated production system in the world (for making ships' rigging pulley blocks), but he was later involved in a number of unprofitable projects. By 1821 he was deep in debt and was tried and committed to debtors' prison in Southwark, where he spent 88 days, only being released after the intervention of the Duke of Wellington. Marc Isambard Brunel's most famous project was the Thames Tunnel (1825-1843) – the first tunnel constructed beneath a navigable river. Originally designed for horse-drawn carriages, it was first used by trains in 1869 and is now part of the London Overground railway network, and is the oldest tunnel in the oldest metro system in the world.

Isambard Kingdom Brunel was even more famous than his father; he built dockyards and the fastest railway in the world, the 7ft broad gauge Great Western; constructed a series of steamships, including the first propeller-driven transatlantic steamship; and engineered numerous important bridges and tunnels. His designs revolutionised public transport and modern engineering.

This museum has a riverside terrace and gardens, a café and a bookshop.

> On Sunday mornings and Tuesday evenings (and advertised days), the museum opens a 'secret' underground chamber where Isambard Kingdom Brunel nearly drowned.

Address: **Borough High Street, SE1 1JA (020-7357 7331, stgeorge-themartyr.co.uk)**

Opening hours: **Contact church for opening hours. Free concerts on Thu at 1pm and other times. See website for concert and service times.**

Cost: **free**

Transport: **Borough tube**

ST GEORGE THE MARTYR

St George the Martyr is a beautiful church in historic Borough and is believed to be the first church in London dedicated to Saint George. The earliest reference to the church is in the annals of Bermondsey Abbey, which records that it was the gift of Thomas de Arderne and his son in 1122. Little is known about the original Norman church, which was rebuilt at the end of the 14th century. The second church appears on some early maps of Southwark and can be seen in William Hogarth's painting *Southwark Fair* in 1733, after which the church was again demolished and replaced with the current structure in 1736, designed by John Price.

St George's is built of red brick with Portland stone dressings, with the west tower faced wholly in stone. The main roof is covered with copper in place of the former slated roof; only the roof over the sanctuary is now slated. The church has galleries on three sides fronted with plain oak panelling, under which the plaster ceiling is recessed with simple coved mouldings to allow more light from the lower windows. The building has retained its Georgian appearance, although a spectacular new ceiling was designed in 1897 in an Italianate style by Basil Champneys (1842-1935). Other notable features include the 18th-century font, the lead cistern, the Little Dorrit vestry, the superb east window, the 18th-century steeple clock with four dials, and the organ, containing some 200 pipes over 300 years old, thought to have been made by Father Smith (1630-1708).

Among the famous people associated with St George's are poet John Gower (1330-1408), who was a benefactor; Peter Carmelianus (d 1527 – poet and Latin scholar to Henry VII) who was rector; and Nahum

> Charles Dickens (1812-1870) had close ties with the parish and church – his father was imprisoned for debt in neighbouring Marshalsea prison, of which a surviving wall lies at the north side of the churchyard – and he set several scenes in his novel *Little Dorrit* (1857) in and around St George's.

Tate (1652-1715), author of the carol *While Shepherds Watched Their Flocks By Night* (who was buried here).

Between 2005 and 2007 the church underwent major restoration, which rebuilt and reinforced the foundations and transformed the crypt into an attractive and spacious community resource. Today St George's stands in the midst of a dynamic area of regeneration and change, at a junction where Roman, medieval and modern roads have converged for 2,000 years.

Address: **St Thomas' Hospital, 2 Lambeth Palace Road, SE1 7EW (020-7188 4400, florence-nightingale.co.uk)**

Opening hours: **10am-5pm**

Cost: **adults £8, children & concessions £6, families £17**

Transport: **Waterloo, Lambeth North or Westminster tube**

- 234 -

FLORENCE NIGHTINGALE MUSEUM

The Florence Nightingale Museum tells the engrossing story of the life of one of Britain's greatest heroines. From the slate she used as a child, her pet owl Athena and the Turkish lantern she used in the Crimean War, the collection spans the life of Florence Nightingale (1820-1910) and her nursing legacy.

Nightingale was born in Florence (after which she was named) on 12th May 1820, the daughter of wealthy landowner William Nightingale. At 17 she felt called by God to some unnamed great cause and despite her domineering mother's persistent attempts, refused to marry several worthy suitors. At the age of 25, Florence told her parents she wanted to become a nurse, to which they were totally opposed, as nursing was then associated with working class women. However, Florence persisted and in 1851, at the age of 31, her father gave his permission and she travelled to Kaiserswerth, Germany, where she studied to become a nurse at the Institute of Protestant Deaconesses.

Two years later Florence was appointed resident lady superintendent of a hospital for invalid women in Harley Street, W1. The same year the Crimean War began, and there were soon reports describing the desperate lack of proper medical facilities and care for wounded soldiers at the front. In 1854, Florence led a team of 38 nurses who cared for thousands of soldiers during the war and helped save the British army from medical disaster.

She returned to England in 1856 and in 1860 established the Nightingale Training School for nurses at London's St Thomas' Hospital, now affiliated to King's College. Once trained, nurses were sent to hospitals throughout Britain, where they introduced Nightingale's ideas and

> It was in the Crimea that Florence was dubbed 'The Lady with the Lamp' after her habit of making rounds at night with a lantern.

established nursing training. Her theories, published in *Notes on Nursing* (1860), were hugely influential and her concerns for sanitation, military health and hospital planning established practices which are still in use today.

Florence was also a visionary health reformer, a brilliant campaigner and the second most influential woman in Victorian Britain and its Empire, after Queen Victoria herself. Her ideas completely changed society's approach to nursing and her legacy remains strong to this day. The Nightingale Pledge taken by new nurses was named in her honour, and International Nurses Day is celebrated throughout the world on her birthday. She died on 13th August 1910, aged 90.

AT A GLANCE

Address: 65-67 Peckham Road, SE5 8UH (020-7703 6120, southlondongallery.org)

Opening hours: Tue-Sun 11am-6pm (Wed and last Fri of the month until 9pm), closed Mon

Cost: free

Transport: Oval or Victoria tube then 36 or 436 bus (alight at Peckham Road/Southampton Way)

SOUTH LONDON GALLERY

The South London Gallery (or SLG, as it's widely known) is a publicly-funded gallery of contemporary art in Camberwell. It was founded in 1891, when it was called the South London Fine Art Gallery. But the gallery's origins go back to the South London Working Men's College in Blackfriars Road in 1868, whose principal was the biologist Thomas Henry Huxley (1825-1895), the grandfather of *Brave New World* author Aldous Huxley. Leading artists such as Sir Frederic Leighton (President of the Royal Academy), Edward Burne-Jones and G. F. Watts supported the fledgling gallery, and Prime Minister William Ewart Gladstone was its first president, succeeded by Leighton in 1887.

During its formative years it moved to the site of a free library, and continued to occupy various South London locations until moving to its current, purpose-built home constructed of Portland stone and hand-made pressed bricks, much favoured by the Arts and Crafts tradition of the time. The original marquetry floor (not on public display) was designed by Walter Crane and bears the inscription 'The source of art is in the life of a people.' In 1893, a lecture hall and library were added, funded by newspaper owner John Passmore Edwards (1823-1911) and officially opened by the Prince of Wales (now demolished after being badly damaged in World War Two).

The gallery staged a changing programme of fine and applied arts' exhibitions and began to form a collection from works donated by artists and subscribers. It has grown over the gallery's lifetime and now includes works by modern

> The SLG has an international reputation for its programme of contemporary art exhibitions and live art events, with education projects for children, young people and adults.

British artists, a collection of over five hundred 20th-century prints and contemporary works relating to South London. Although the collection isn't on permanent display, it's a valuable resource for school projects, giving students hands-on experience of contemporary works of art.

The gallery's profile and visitor numbers have grown in recent decades as it began to stage exhibitions by internationally acclaimed artists such as Gilbert & George, Anselm Kiefer and Sherrie Levine, as well as younger artists such as Tracey Emin, Gavin Turk and Ann Sofi-Sidén. In 2010, the gallery opened additional buildings designed by 6a Architects to provide new small-scale galleries, an artists' flat, an excellent café, gardens, and an education and events studio on the footprint of the original lecture hall. The Matsudaira Wing, Clore Studio and Fox Garden opened to the public in 2010.

Address: **Norwood Road, SE27 9JU (020-7926 7999,**
westnorwoodcemetery.org, fownc.org)

Opening hours: **Apr-Oct, Mon-Fri 8am-6pm, Sat-Sun 10am-6pm (Nov-Mar**
closes at 4pm)

Cost: **free**

Transport: **West Norwood rail**

WEST NORWOOD CEMETERY

West Norwood Cemetery is a site of major historical, architectural and ecological interest, yet many people have never heard of it. It was built by the South Metropolitan Cemetery Company and opened in 1837, the second of London's 'Magnificent Seven' cemeteries created in the 1830s and 1840s to solve London's chronic lack of burial grounds. The cemetery, now owned by Lambeth Borough Council, covers 40 acres (16ha), was the first British cemetery to be designed in the Gothic Revival style and is considered one of the most significant in Europe.

West Norwood Cemetery offered a rural setting in open countryside, as it lay outside London at that time, and its design and location attracted wealthy Victorians, who commissioned fine mausoleums and memorials for their burial plots and vaults. Today the grounds are a mixture of historic monumental cemetery and modern lawn cemetery, but it also contains catacombs, cremation plots, a columbarium for cinerary ashes and a memorial garden. There were originally two chapels, the Dissenters Chapel and the Episcopal Chapel (both with catacombs beneath them); the latter was badly damaged in World War Two and demolished in 1955.

In 1842, a section of the cemetery was acquired by London's Greek community for a Greek Orthodox necropolis, which soon filled with grand monuments and large mausoleums (18 of which are listed),

> Among the most famous monuments is the mausoleum for Sir Henry Doulton's family, constructed appropriately of pottery and terracotta. Other notable memorials include Mrs Beeton (cookery books), Dr William Marsden (surgeon), Sir Hiram Stevens Maxim (inventor of the Maxim gun), Baron Julius de Reuter (founder of the Reuters news agency), Charles Spurgeon (preacher) and Sir Henry Tate (sugar merchant/Tate Gallery).

memorialising the history of Anglo-Hellenic families. Considered to contain the best collection of sepulchral monuments in London, the cemetery has 65 Grade II and Grade II* listed buildings and structures (more than any other cemetery), including the entrance arch and railings.

By the '60s the cemetery had become neglected and overgrown, and in 1966 it was purchased by Lambeth Council, which maintained the cremation service and converted the grounds into a memorial park. The cemetery contains a wide variety of trees (including many rare species) and shrubs (bramble, ivy, rose and hawthorn), while in the spring there are daffodils, wild primroses and bluebells. The grounds are a haven for wildlife such as foxes, squirrels and numerous bird species, including willow warblers, kestrels and tawny owls.

Address: Thicket Road, SE20 8DT (0300-303 8658, crystalpalacepark.org.
uk, cpdinosaurs.org)

Opening hours: Mon-Fri 7.30am-dusk, Sat-Sun 9am-dusk

Cost: free

Transport: Crystal Palace rail

CRYSTAL PALACE PARK & DINOSAURS

Crystal Palace Park is a historic pleasure ground used for a wide variety of cultural and sporting events. It's run by the borough of Bromley and gets its name from the Crystal Palace, a cast-iron and glass building, originally erected in Hyde Park to house the Great Exhibition of 1851. Following the exhibition, the palace was moved and reconstructed in 1854 in a modified and enlarged form in Penge Place estate at Sydenham Hill (one of the highest points in London, 357ft/109m above sea level), which led to the local area being dubbed Crystal Palace – now named Crystal Palace Park. The Palace attracted visitors for over seven decades until being destroyed by fire in 1936 (two Sphinx statues survive).

The grounds surrounding the Palace were extensively renovated and turned into a public park, with ornamental gardens, replicas of statues and two man-made lakes. In 1852, Benjamin Waterhouse Hawkins (1807-1894) was commissioned to build the first ever life-sized models of extinct animals, which he did under the guidance of Sir Richard Owen (1804-1892) – who invented the word 'dinosaur' – a celebrated biologist and palaeontologist. Their importance lies in being the first attempt to interpret what full-scale prehistoric animals would have looked like, based on the best scientific information available at the time. Unveiled in 1854, they were the first dinosaur sculptures (15 still exist) in the world, pre-dating the publication of Charles Darwin's *On the Origin of Species* by five years.

As further discoveries of dinosaurs were made, the models' reputation declined, and by 1895 experts looked on them with scorn and ridicule. Nevertheless, the dinosaurs (Grade I listed) continue to capture the

The park once housed a football ground that hosted the FA Cup final from 1895 to 1914, as well as staging London County Cricket games from 1900 to 1908 (WG Grace played here).

imagination of both young and old, and were extensively restored in 2003, when the anatomical errors were retained to maintain authenticity with the Victorian originals.

The extensive grounds were used in pre-war days for motorcycle and, after the '50s, car racing – known as the Crystal Palace circuit – which fell into disuse in 1973. The site is now home to the National Sports Centre, built in 1964, and also contains a boating lake, maze (the Tea Maze is London's largest), museum, pool with flamingos, children's playground, concert area, an urban farm, café and the Crystal Palace TV transmitting station, the third-tallest structure in London (719ft/219m).

CROSSNESS PUMPING STATION

The Crossness Pumping Station (Grade I listed) was built by Sir Joseph William Bazalgette (1819-1891) and architect Charles Henry Driver (1832-1900) as part of Victorian London's main sewerage system – officially opened by the Prince of Wales in April 1865. In the early 19th century, London's water supply and the Thames were heavily polluted with sewage, which resulted in several cholera outbreaks during which up to 20,000 people died annually.

Joseph Bazalgette was one of the most distinguished Victorian civil engineers, and after being employed on various railway projects he was appointed chief engineer of the Metropolitan Board of Works in 1855, having previously worked for the Metropolitan Commission of Sewers. Bazalgette built 83 miles (134km) of 'interceptory' sewers that prevented raw sewage from running into the Thames and took it to the east of London where it was pumped into the river with minimal effect on the population. This system involved four major pumping stations, at Abbey Mills (in the Lea Valley), Chelsea (close to today's Grosvenor Bridge), Deptford and Crossness on the Erith marshes.

At Crossness Pumping Station, the Beam Engine House was constructed in the Romanesque (Norman) style in gault (clay) brick, with considerable ornamentation, red brick arches and dog-tooth string courses. The interior features spectacular, colourful ornate Victorian wrought and cast ironwork and was described as "A masterpiece of engineering – a Victorian cathedral of ironwork" by architectural expert Nikolaus Pevsner. It contains the four original pumping engines, which are possibly the largest remaining rotative beam engines in the world, with 52-ton flywheels and 47-ton beams. Although modern diesel engines were subsequently introduced, the old beam engines remained in service until work on a new sewerage treatment plant began in 1956.

The Crossness Engines Trust was created in 1987 to restore the installation, which is a unique part of Britain's industrial heritage and an outstanding example of Victorian engineering. The spectacular building, engines and pumps are a monument to Bazalgette's genius in solving London's problems: he was also responsible for the Thames Embankments; Battersea, Hammersmith and Putney Bridges; and many of London's other capital projects.

> The 'Great Stink' of 1858 – when the Houses of Parliament became so smelly that members demanded action – was the catalyst for the creation of London's sewerage system, which remains in use today.

Address: Bourne Road, Bexley, DA5 1PQ (01322-526574, hallplace.org.uk)

Opening hours: house 10am-5pm (closed on bank holidays), gardens Apr-Sep 9am-10pm, Oct-Mar 9am-4pm

Cost: adults £10, concessions £9, children £5, families £24.50

Transport: Bexley rail

HALL PLACE & GARDENS

Hall Place (Grade I listed) is a former stately home on a beautiful 160-acre (65ha) estate, sitting beside the River Cray on the outskirts of Crayford (Bexley). The house dates to around 1537, when wealthy merchant Sir John Champneys, former Lord Mayor of London, used stone recycled from nearby Lesnes Abbey to build a country house. In 1649, the house was sold to another wealthy merchant, Sir Robert Austen (1587-1666), who added a second wing made of red brick – doubling the size of the house, but without trying to harmonise the two parts – which are constructed in highly contrasting architectural styles.

The house remained in the Austen family until the mid-18th century, when Robert Austen (1697-1743), the 4th baronet, died. The estate was purchased in around 1772 by his brother-in-law, Sir Francis Dashwood (1708-1781), founder of the notorious Hellfire Club. For much of the 19th and early 20th centuries the house was let to various tenants, although it remained in the Dashwood family until 1926. The borough of Bexley became the owner of the estate and Hall Place in 1935.

Much of the house that Sir John built still survives. Constructed on a traditional, hierarchical plan, the core of the house consisted of a splendid central great hall with a minstrels' gallery, crossed at one end by a service wing and the other by high status family accommodation, including a parlour and great chamber. The outer walls are a distinctive chequerboard pattern made of flint and rubble masonry, a beautiful example of the Tudor love of pattern. The 17th-century additions and improvements by Sir Robert Austen include a vaulted Long Gallery and a spectacular Great Chamber with a fine plaster ceiling.

> The visitor centre offers a riverside café, pub and restaurant (in the estate's Jacobean barn), plus a gift shop.

Surrounding the house are award-winning formal gardens, including a stunning topiary lawn of chess pieces and the topiary Queen's Beasts, planted for the coronation of Queen Elizabeth II. There are also enclosed gardens, rose and herb gardens, and inspirational herbaceous borders, while the walled garden has a sub-tropical plant house where bananas ripen in mid-winter. The parkland, through which the River Cray flows, contains an exceptional variety of trees and an abundance of wildlife.

An extensive programme of events, family activities, concerts and theatre is organised in the house and gardens, while displays include the house's history and exhibits from Bexley's museum collection, plus contemporary art exhibitions.

Address: Luxted Road, Downe, BR6 7JT (01689-859119, english-heritage.org.uk/visit/places/home-of-charles-darwin-down-house)

Opening hours: winter/spring (Nov-Mar), weekends 10am-4pm, summer/autumn (Apr-Oct) daily 10am-6pm (see website for exact dates and times)

Cost: adults £12.70, concessions £11.40, children £7.60, families (2 adults, three children) £33. Free to English Heritage members.

Transport: Bromley South rail then 146 bus

Charles Darwin

DOWN HOUSE (HOME OF CHARLES DARWIN)

Down House and its 18-acre (7.2ha) estate was the home of the renowned English naturalist Charles Darwin (1809-1882) and his family, from 1842 until his death 40 years later. Its history can be traced to 1651, when Thomas Manning sold a parcel of land to John Know the elder, who built the first house. The house passed through several hands and was rebuilt and enlarged in the 18th century by George Butler, a businessman and landowner, when it was called the Great House. In 1837, it was renovated under the supervision of Edward Cresy, a local architect, until being purchased by Charles Darwin in 1842.

When he moved to Down House with his young family, it was a plain and sturdy 18th-century block. Darwin made extensive alterations to the house and grounds, particularly during the first five years he lived here, extending and enlarging it with a new service wing. Darwin's wife, Emma, bore him ten children, of whom three died young, but the surviving five boys and two girls flourished at Down.

Situated in rural Kent (now the London borough of Bromley), the house offered the peace and privacy that Darwin needed to work on his revolutionary scientific theories. It was at Down (and its 'open-air laboratory') that he developed his landmark views on evolution by natural selection and wrote his groundbreaking work, *On the Origin of Species* (1859) – a book that shook the Victorian world and which has influenced scientific thinking ever since.

After the death of Emma in 1896, the house was let on a series of short-term tenancies, except for the period 1907-1921 when it was a girls' school. It then languished empty for a number of years, until Sir Arthur Keith (1866-

> The house and grounds were extensively restored by English Heritage to their 'original' state during Darwin's time and opened to the public in 1998.

1955), curator of the Hunterian Museum, encouraged the British Association for the Advancement of Science (BAAS) to preserve it as a national memorial to Darwin. Down House was maintained as a museum by the BAAS for 60 years, until in 1996 the house and its contents were purchased by English Heritage (ER) with support from the Wellcome Trust and Heritage Lottery Fund.

Today you can see Darwin's famous study and stroll through the extensive gardens that inspired the great scientist.

Address: 20 Montford Place, SE11 5DE (020-7587 0034, beefeaterdistillery. com)

Opening hours: Mon-Sat 10am-6.30pm, closed Sun; tours hourly 11am-5pm

Cost: tours £15 (1½ hours), VIP experience £40 (2½ hours)

Transport: Oval or Kennington tube

BEEFEATER GIN DISTILLERY

Beefeater's history can be traced back to 1862 when James Burrough bought the Cale Street (Chelsea) distillery from John Taylor and began to produce his own distinctive style of gin. By 1876 the company had an increasing portfolio of gins with brand names such as Ye Old Chelsea and James Burrough London Dry, as well as Old Tom styles. By experimenting, inventing and using new processes Burrough discovered that blending a particular recipe of botanicals produced a bold, full-flavoured gin, which he named Beefeater Gin. After its almost instant success, it quickly became the company's flagship product.

The original Beefeater recipe book dated 1895, specifies that nine botanicals are essential (juniper, angelica root, angelica seeds, coriander seeds, liquorice, almonds, orris root, Seville oranges and lemon peel) to create the gin's full-bodied and robust flavour. As James Burrough's company rapidly expanded and needed to increase its distilling capacity, a new Beefeater distillery was built in Lambeth in 1908. Beefeater production moved again in 1958 to its current home in Kennington, where still manufacturer John Dore was commissioned to create a larger set of copper stills mimicking those of the former Chelsea Distillery. Today the method of steeping and distilling devised by James Burrough in the 1860s (along with the secret recipe he created) remains virtually unchanged. Beefeater remained a family business until 1987, when it was sold to Whitbread, then to Allied Domecq and current owners Pernod Ricard in 2005.

The Beefeater visitor centre opened in 2014 and allows you to see the original stills, view the distilling process and learn about the company's history. A self-discovery tour

> Beefeater gin is exported to over 100 countries across the globe, with annual sales of over 2.3 million nine-litre cases, all of which is produced with fewer than ten employees at the Kennington Distillery.

takes you on a journey through the history of gin ('mother's ruin') in London and explores how international politics, exotic imports from the British Empire, an era of Victorian entrepreneurs and some savvy American barmen made gin the world's favourite cocktail spirit. The tour takes you to the heart of the distillery to learn about the hand-crafted production process and experience a sensory understanding of the ingredients used to create Beefeater gin. Last but not least, you enjoy a tutored comparative tasting of some of Beefeater's gins, culminating in a complimentary gin and tonic. Cheers!

London's Architectural Walks, 2nd Edition

ISBN: 978-1-913171-01-8, 128 pages, softback, £9.99, Jim Watson

London's Architectural Walks is a unique guide to the most celebrated landmark buildings in one of the world's major cities. In thirteen easy walks, it takes you on a fascinating journey through London's diverse architectural heritage with historical background and clear maps. Some of the capital's most beautiful parks are visited, plus palaces, theatres, museums and some surprising oddities.

The author's line and watercolour illustrations of all the city's significant buildings, make London's Architectural Walks an essential companion for anyone interested in the architecture that has shaped this great metropolis.

London's Secret Walks, 3rd Edition

ISBN: 978-1-909282-99-5, 320 pages, softback, £10.99
David Hampshire

London is a great city for walking – whether for pleasure, exercise or simply to get from A to B. Despite the city's extensive public transport system, walking is often the quickest and most enjoyable way to get around – at least in the centre – and it's also free and healthy! Many attractions are off the beaten track, away from the major thoroughfares and public transport hubs. This favours walking as the best way to explore them, as does the fact that London is a visually interesting city with a wealth of stimulating sights in every 'nook and cranny'.

London's Waterside Walks

ISBN: 978-1-909282-96-4, 192 pages, softback, £9.99
David Hampshire

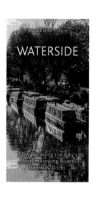

Most people are familiar with London's River Thames, but the city has much more to offer when it comes to waterways, including a wealth of canals, minor rivers (most are tributaries of the Thames), former docklands, lakes and reservoirs. London's Waterside Walks takes you along many of the city's lesser-known, hidden waterways.

INDEX

N/O

P

R

S

T

U/V

W

Y

Great British Weekend Escapes

ISBN: 978-1-913171-21-6, 224 pages, softback, £10.99, David Hampshire, summer 2020

When you want to escape for a few days, Britain offers a wealth of cities and towns where you can treat yourself to a well-deserved break at any time of the year. *Great British Weekend Escapes* contains 70 enticing getaways, from the tourist hotspots of London and Liverpool to Edinburgh and Manchester, Glasgow to York; the enchanting university cities of Cambridge and Oxford; awe-inspiring cathedral cities such as Durham and Ely, Lincoln and Winchester; and captivating small towns like Rye, Southwold and Whitby.

Touring the Lake District

ISBN: 978-1-913171-22-3, 128 pages, softback, £9.99, Jim Watson, summer 2020

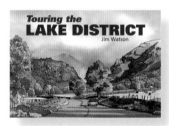

Touring the Lake District is a unique illustrated guide to exploring the area by car. Eight carefully planned tours take in the popular tourist centres plus a wealth of hidden gems many consider to be the 'Real Lakeland'. The tours visit most of the famous lakes, negotiate empty country lanes, cross open moorland and test your driving skills on mountain passes. With picturesque villages, award-winning gastro pubs and rustic coffee shops to enjoy along the routes, this book will provide you with a comprehensive portrait of this varied and magnificent region.

Touring the Cotswolds

ISBN: 978-1-909282-91-9, 128 pages, softback, £9.99, Jim Watson

Touring the Cotswolds is a unique guide to exploring the best of the Cotswolds by car through eight carefully planned tours that take in the heavyweight tourist centres plus a wealth of hidden gems (the 'real Cotswolds'). You'll negotiate a maze of country lanes, high hills with panoramic views, lush woodlands and beautiful valleys, plus an abundance of picturesque villages, providing a comprehensive portrait of this varied and delightful area.

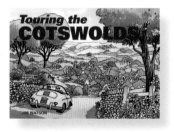

see citybooks.co

London's Green Walks

London's Green Walks

ISBN: 978-1-909282-82-7, softback, 192 pages, £9.99
David Hampshire

Green spaces cover almost 40 per cent of Greater London, ranging from magnificent royal parks and garden cemeteries, full of intrigue and history, to majestic ancient forests and barely tamed heathland; from elegant squares and formal country parks to enchanting 'secret' gardens. The 20 walks take in famous destinations, such as Hyde Park and Regent's Park, but also many smaller and lesser known – but no less beautiful – parks and gardens, all of which are free to explore.

London's Village Walks

ISBN: 978-1-909282-94-0, softback, 192 pages, £9.99
David Hampshire

From its beginnings as a Roman trading port some 2,000 years ago, London has mushroomed into the metropolis we see today, swallowing up thousands of villages, hamlets and settlements in the process. Nevertheless, if you're seeking a village vibe you can still find it if you know where to look. Scratch beneath the surface of modern London and you'll find a rich tapestry of ancient villages, just waiting to be rediscovered.

London's Village Walks

London's Monumental Walks

London's Monumental Walks

ISBN: 978-1-909282-95-7, softback, 192 pages, £9.99
David Hampshire

It isn't perhaps surprising that in a city as rich in history as London, there's a wealth of public monuments, statues and memorials: in fact London probably has more statues than any other world city. Its streets, squares, parks and gardens are crammed with monuments to kings and queens, military heroes, politicians and local worthies, artists and writers, and notables from every walk of life (plus a few that commemorate deeds and people best forgotten), along with a wealth of abstract and contemporary works of art.

Peaceful London, 2nd edition

ISBN: 978-1-909282-84-1, 192 pages, softback, £9.99, David Hampshire

Whether you're seeking a place to recharge your batteries, rest your head, revive your spirits, restock your larder or refuel your body; somewhere to inspire, soothe or uplift your mood; or just wish to discover a part of London that's a few steps further off the beaten track, *Peaceful London* will steer you in the right direction.

Quirky London, 2nd edition

ISBN: 978-1-909282-98-8, 192 pages, softback, £9.99, David Hampshire

The British are noted for their eccentricities and London is no exception, with an abundance of bizarre and curious places and stories. *Quirky London* explores over 300 of the city's more unusual places and sights that often fail to register on the radar of both visitors and residents alike.

London Escapes

ISBN: 978-1-913171-00-1, 192 pages, softback, £10.99 David Hampshire

London offers a wealth of attractions, but sometimes you just want to escape the city's constant hustle and bustle and visit somewhere with a gentler, slower pace of life. *London Escapes* offers over 70 days out, from historical towns and lovely villages to magnificent stately homes and gardens; beautiful, nostalgic seaside resorts and beaches to spectacular parks and nature reserves.

see citybooks.co